ALLENDE

PINOCHET

Two Political Dramas

Peter Turton

Books

Managing Editors: Cliff Clark and Sam Pearson
Cover Design: Alisha Anderson

Published in the United States by CBH Books.
CBH Books is a division of Cambridge BrickHouse, Inc.

Cambridge BrickHouse, Inc.
60 Island Street
Lawrence, MA 01840 U.S.A.

Library of Congress Catalog No. 2007006208
ISBN 978-1-59835-045-6
First Edition

Printed in Canada
10 9 8 7 6 5 4 3 2 1

ALLENDE

Peter Turton

To Salvador Allende, People's Unity, and their allies

CONTENTS

'Let them know this, let them hear this very clearly, let it make a deep impression on them: I shall defend this Chilean revolution and I shall defend the People's government. The people have given me their mandate; I have no alternative. Only by riddling me with bullets will they be able to end our will to carry out the people's program'.

-Allende's speech at the National Stadium, Santiago de Chile, 4 December 1971

PROLOGUE

Scene 1 *September 14, 1970. Washington, D.C., USA. A meeting of the 40 Committee, presided over by Henry Kissinger, U.S. National Security Adviser to President Richard Nixon. Kissinger wears large spectacles and has a marked German accent.*

Dr. Salvador Allende, a longstanding Marxist politician, a Mason, and an atheist, after standing unsuccessfully as a presidential candidate several times, has finally won, ten days previously, the Chilean presidential election at the head of a coalition of left parties called People's Unity. Allende's victory over the second candidate, Jorge Alessandri of the right-wing National Party, is only by a very slim margin (1.5%), and in any case he has not obtained the more than 50% of the votes necessary for him to be automatically inaugurated as President. A third candidate, Radomiro Tomic of the Christian Democratic Party, has won over a quarter of the total vote. In these cases it is the custom for the Chilean Congress to decide by vote who will be the next President, before the following 24 October. Kissinger and his colleagues are worried, because it seems that the Congress will confirm Allende's presidency.

KISSINGER   Gentlemen, the situation in Chile is

serious. I don't see why we need to stand by and watch a country go communist due to the irresponsibility of its own people. We have already spent $11 million to prevent this man from coming to power, between 1962 and now.

COMMITTEE MEMBER ONE But Allende has to be confirmed by their Congress, doesn't he?

KISSINGER Sure. But that's what is most likely to happen. There'll be a run-off between Allende and Allessandri, and a big proportion of the Christian Democratic congressmen will side with Allende's leftists. He only needs 101 votes out of the total number of congressmen, which is 200. Tomic, the Christian Democrat leader, made a pact with Allende that if either of them won the first election, the other would vote for him in Congress. A lot of the Christian Democrats like Allende. They think he's a 'respectable' Marxist, being somewhat of a gentleman. And he's been around for a long time. He has prestige. He was the leader of the Chilean Senate. In my book, there's no such thing as a 'respectable' Marxist. Even if Allende is one of them, he will open the door for the rest to pour through. He's a friend of Fidel Castro, also. Need I say more?

COMMITTEE MEMBER TWO President Frei doesn't want Allende as his successor. He might use his office and the Chilean military to stop him.

KISSINGER Perhaps. And there is a legal loophole that might serve us. The Chilean Congress is actually not required to confirm its own majority vote in these circumstances. It does so customarily, but in fact does not have to by law.

COMMITTEE MEMBER THREE What is the position of the Chilean Armed Forces, sir?

KISSINGER Traditionally, they go along with the decision of their Congress. Chile is not a banana republic. Their military have a good record of playing second fiddle to the politicians. The Commander-in-Chief of the Army, General Schneider, has confirmed this. He has stated that he will respect any decision taken by Congress.

COMMITTEE MEMBER ONE If only we could get Alessandri elected by Congress by using our money. I'm sure those Chilean congressmen aren't any more virtuous than our own. It will take a lot of money, though, even for us. If Alessandri were elected by their Congress, we could get him to resign, and Frei could call a second presidential election to be fought by two candidates, not three. The National Party and the Christian Democrats could field a common candidate against our gentleman communist, and we would be home. The left would scream, but what could they do? The Armed Forces would keep the lid on the situation. Let's try that.

KISSINGER Sounds like a good idea. What kind of money would go in the pot? A quarter of a million?

COMMITTEE MEMBER TWO Yes, sir, that would be enough.

KISSINGER It doesn't seem very much. Those Chileans are cheap. All the better for us. Can I take it this sum is approved? There may be more money from private sources. The International Telephone and Telegraph people are prepared to give a seven-figure sum to stop Allende. I am putting the plan to the vote.

ALL [*raising their hands*] Approved.

KISSINGER It's not only the money. Frei must not *allow* large sections of his party to vote for Allende. Use his authority. Can he do that?

AIDE Well, he's our man, sir. Ever since the days of Kennedy we have backed the Christian Democrats in Latin America, and Frei's already had a load of our money for his party to keep the leftists out. He should keep his pants on about the possibility of a coup.

KISSINGER So he should. But will he? I'm adjourning the meeting. Tomorrow I have to see President Nixon, the director of the CIA and the Attorney General about this situation. The President wants Allende stopped by any means possible. I'll report back to this committee as soon as possible.

Scene 2 *The same committee, meeting on September 29. Kissinger has now been promoted to Secretary of State.*

KISSINGER Gentlemen, the pace around this Chilean imbroglio is heating up. The President's worried, and so is the CIA. Richard Helms thinks big spending is necessary to stop Beelzebub. He wants maximum effort, and contingency plans for the scenario if Allende does get confirmed by the Chilean Congress. If that happens, he says we should make their economy scream. My doubts about Frei have been confirmed, by the way. We've heard that the Chilean Armed Forces are quite aware of the threat from Allende, and they don't want him as President. But they will only go ahead with the green light from Frei, and he is now saying he wants Allende blocked constitutionally. In other words, the election of Alessandri.

COMMITTEE MEMBER ONE And if their Congress elects Allende? What then?

KISSINGER We'll have lost the first round. That's why we're going to draw up urgent contingency plans. It seems that the Chilean Armed Forces are not going to act unilaterally unless Allende's confirmation creates extreme instability. Anyway, in the meantime, we're pulling out all the stops. We're flooding the Chilean media with anti-Allende propaganda, through *El Mercurio* and the hostile radio and TV stations. Funded by CIA and ITT money. We've thought about a run on their banks to create chaos before their congressional decision. That might put them off electing the comrade. We're infiltrating their extreme left to produce more unrest. Ambassador Kerry sees General Schneider as an obstacle. He advises getting him out of the way. We've already warned Frei that if Allende does get in, we'll take all the economic measures we can to wreck the country and make it look like an emerging communist state.

AIDE Allende's ploy to the democrats is the 'peaceful road to socialism' strictly within the bounds of the constitution. In all other countries, the Marxists have only come to power by violent revolution and they've never been forced out of power subsequently. But nearly half of Chile is opposed to him. It'll be difficult for him and his successors to hang onto power.

KISSINGER Well, gentlemen, we're certainly not going to help him. I don't think he has any supporters in Washington. [*Members of the committee chortle.*] The Armed Forces are the key. Most of the big brass are Frei people, or even more anti-communist. Allende's going to have a lot on his plate. In fact, I'm rather glad I'm not him. He doesn't know what he's getting himself into. I can almost relish him being confirmed as Chile's first 'comrade president'. Perhaps it's rather nice for us that Frei has turned out to have no balls. If he wants to play the Latin American democrat, let him. Now, gentlemen, let's move on to other business.

ACT 1

Scene 1 *November 5. Allende has been confirmed as President by the Chilean Congress and is making his inaugural speech from the National Stadium in Santiago. A group of working-class, politically active Chileans are gathered together in the home of one of them to listen to Allende's speech on the radio.*

MIGUEL   Well, old Chicho finally made it. What was it? His fourth or fifth go?

DANIEL   He tried in '52, '58, and '64. So it's fourth time lucky.

MIGUEL   Don't say lucky. He deserved to be elected. I'm optimistic. People's Unity is strong and has a lot of support from Tomic's part of the Christian Democrats. Allende really wants to change things for people like us. Now he has the power to do so. Of course, he's a bourgeois. He likes his whisky and has an eye for the ladies. But he's decent and honorable.

ANA   Too right he's a bourgeois, an armchair Marxist. Who was it Congress asked to welcome the Queen of England when she came here? He won't really change things for the working class, even if they let him have a go. We need a real revolution here, and that means the armed struggle, like in Cuba.

DANIEL You hotheads in the MIR are going to wreck everything. Chile is not Cuba. We have a big middle class here and they can't stand the word 'revolution'. And behind the middle class is the military. Do you think they like the People's Unity program? 'Building socialism in democracy, pluralism, and freedom.' Allende has to be very careful not to step over the line of legality. And all your party talks of is 'the armed struggle'. That line is inviting the military to take over. Do you really think you can beat them in a civil war, which is what your party appears to want?

ANA It'll come down to that in the end, so we might as well prepare for it now. But remember, most people in the Armed Forces are workers. Some of the high command have sympathies for the left, also. My party plans to do much propaganda work amongst the military.

DANIEL Yes, I've heard all that talk about infiltration. But it's just schoolboy talk. Your party is just students and riff-raff.

ANA You know that the MIR supplied some of Allende's personal bodyguard. One of his nephews is a leader in our party.

DANIEL [*turning up the radio*] Alright, alright. Let's hear what the man himself has to say.

ALLENDE'S VOICE 'In the words of Engels: "It is possible to conceive of the peaceful evolution of the old society towards the new, in countries where the representation of the people concentrates in itself all the power by which, according to the Constitution, it is possible to do whatever is wanted, from the moment that it has the majority of the nation behind it."'

MIGUEL There you are, my girl. He's quoting Engels.

ANA Engels was wrong. He never really understood Marx, who was quite clear that one class cannot overthrow another except by armed revolution.

MIGUEL We'll see.

ALLENDE'S VOICE 'The Christian Democratic Party has been conscious of the historic moment and of its obligations towards the country, and this must be emphasized.'

MIGUEL Exactly. We knew they would vote for him in Congress. That's why my party's strategy is to forge an alliance with them. We want to take things slowly, not rock the boat. When Frei was President, the right hated the Christian Democrats. It was they that put us on the road to getting our copper back.

ANA You people call yourselves communists, but you're not. The Communist Party here really believes in bourgeois parliamentary democracy because it has a big stake in the system: all those senators and deputies sitting on their fat arses in Congress. You're not revolutionaries at all. You know what Fidel Castro said: 'A revolutionary is the one who makes a revolution.'

MIGUEL We *are* revolutionaries, but we recognize Chilean conditions. The Cubans have to understand that.

ANA The Christian Democrats will eventually betray you. Frei didn't want Allende as President. Neither did Aylwin.

DANIEL [*turning up the radio again*] Listen to what he's saying.

ALLENDE'S VOICE 'I am personally convinced that the heroic sacrifice of a soldier, that of the Commander-in-Chief of the Army, General René Schneider, was the unforeseen event that has saved our country from a civil war.'

MIGUEL You see? Those Fatherland and Freedom fascists didn't manage to provoke the Armed Forces. The military are proud of their tradition of loyalty to the

Constitution. Even Schneider's assassination didn't panic them. And it will stay like that with General Prats in command. He's solid for the Constitution, like Schneider.

ALLENDE'S VOICE 'What is People's Power? People's Power means that we shall demolish the pillars of power of the minorities that have always condemned our country to underdevelopment. We shall put an end to the monopolies, which hand over control of the economy to a few dozen families. We shall put an end to a taxation system at the service of profit and which has always fallen more heavily on the poor than on the rich, and which has concentrated our national savings in the hands of the bankers and their appetite for enrichment. We are going to nationalize credit to put it at the service of the prosperity of the nation and the people. We shall put an end to the huge landed estates, which are continuing to condemn thousands of peasants to submission and extreme poverty, by preventing the country from obtaining all the food that we need from their lands. A real agrarian reform will make this possible.'

DANIEL That's the stuff.

ALLENDE'S VOICE 'We shall recover for Chile its basic riches. We are going to return the large copper, coal, iron, and nitrate mines to our people. We shall do all this by respecting democracy, pluralism, and freedom. Remember what Simón Bolívar said: "If any republic is to survive for a long time in America, I incline to think that it will be the Chilean. There the spirit of freedom has never been extinguished."'

ANA   Bolívar was installing the bourgeoisie in power. And that was a century and a half ago. And now Allende is quoting Bolívar in favour of what he thinks is Marxism. Good God. It's all words, all sleight of hand. Does he really think the big landowners will stand by whilst he expropriates them? Or the banks, when he tries to nationalize them? Or the United States copper companies? Or the Edwards clan? Even if he manages it under the Constitution, legally, they'll never stand for it. He's sitting on a time bomb.

MIGUEL   Well, he'll give it a go. If it fails, it fails. It's never been tried before. We can't be stuck in the past. And this is Chile, the England of South America. Even if there is a mess, it will all get sorted out in the end. We're a civilized country.

ANA   I just hope your optimism is not misplaced. Actually, as you know, my party has resolved to give People's Unity critical support, in spite of our doubts.

MIGUEL   'Critical support'. Typical Trotskyite language. We'll support you because you're in power, then stab you in the back. Your party claims to be a workers' party, but the real workers' parties stick together, present a solid front. There's no room for snipers.

ANA We're not Trotskyites. And we'll see who is who when the right gets going. And your coalition is not very united, is it? Each of the parties has its own agenda and discipline.

MIGUEL You can't have perfection. We're going to do things slowly but surely, within the Constitution. Allende has signed the statutes of guarantees for existing freedom and legalities, including the integrity of the Armed Forces. Allende will stick to them. He's that kind of man. And he won't give up in the face of opposition from the right. He despises it.

ANA You Chilean communists are all the same; conservatives at heart.

DANIEL The MIR will ruin everything. There are many people in my own party like you, unfortunately: the armed struggle brigade.

ANA All you socialists call yourselves Marxists, but the 'armed struggle brigade' people in your party are the only real ones. The rest follow the Allende-Communist Party line of informal alliance with the Christian Democrats. Just see how far it gets you. I have to go now.

MIGUEL   Okay, let's stop bickering. If we quarrel amongst ourselves, the right will end up by making mincemeat of us. [*Ana leaves.*]

DANIEL   She's a nice kid, but so arrogant. Thinks she knows it all.

MIGUEL   Hopelessly idealistic. All those mini Che Guevaras seem to despise us, as if our years of militancy counted for nothing.

DANIEL   Do you think she's really on the same side as us?

MIGUEL   Perhaps. We'll just have to wait and see.

INTERLUDE

A year has gone by and Allende's policies are proving popular with the working classes, as is indicated by the municipal elections of April 1971, when the People's Unity coalition won 50.9% of the vote. Workers' wages and consumption have risen and unemployment has dropped. The first nationalizations of major industries (mainly textiles) have begun. Spontaneous occupations of land by impatient peasants lead to clashes between them and the police. The Chilean Congress has unanimously ratified the copper nationalization bill, in which the former mainly U.S.-owned copper mines have been completely taken over by the Chilean state, with no compensation. However, the right is beginning to show its discontent. Wealthy Santiago housewives stage a 'march of empty cooking pots' in protest against shortages caused by increased demand due to rising wages. Fidel Castro is visiting the country to great popular acclaim and right-wing hostility.

Scene 2 *December 1971. Outside the gates of a large estate in San Fernando, in the Central Valley. Behind the gates can be seen the landowner's large house, with a substantial verandah. Thirty peasants are grouped around a leader. They are carrying spades and hoes.*

PEASANT LEADER Friends, you know why we're

here. We're going in now. Don Samuel should have been taken over years ago. Most of his land is fallow and the pasture is empty since he drove his cattle over to Argentina. He's way over the 200-acre minimum that the Frei people fixed. He wasn't expropriated then because he had connections. And we have practically nothing with large families to feed. The government will support us, you'll see.

PEASANT   Even though we don't have an authorization?

PEASANT LEADER   Look, even the Mapuche Indians are taking over lands when they feel like it. It's illegal, but the government is sympathetic. You're better than a bunch of Indians, aren't you?

[*The landowner appears from out of the house, a large, burly man wearing a hat and boots, accompanied by two men with shotguns.*]

LANDOWNER   You try to get in and we'll shoot.

PEASANT LEADER   [*unfurling a Chilean flag*] This land is ours. It should have been taken over a long time ago. You know what the agrarian reform says. [*To the armed guards*] You're just peasants like us. Why are you slaves to this man? You can't shoot us.

GUARD [*to the landowner*] Don Samuel, there are so many of them. Even if we shoot, they'll overwhelm us.

LANDOWNER What am I paying you for? Don't you and your families live off me?

GUARD It's no use. I don't want to kill anybody. I know most of those people.

LANDOWNER You gutless bastards. Get back into the house. [*They retreat into the house. The peasants cheer and break the gates open. One of them unfurls a Chilean flag and waves it. The peasants rush behind the house and pitch tents on the land.*]

[*Inside the house. The landowner is on the telephone.*]

Prudencio, I want a court order against a mob who are occupying my land illegally. What? It's no use? But they have no papers or anything. It's an invasion. My land has been in my family for centuries. Nothing like this has ever happened before. What? I know the political situation is bad with these communists in power. But I can't let myself be taken over by any filthy rag-tag-and-bobtail. You're a Christian Democrat, aren't you? We have to stick together. Of course I'm National Party, but our cause is the same. You know how Frei hates Allende. Okay, you'll make out an order. Please do. In the meantime, I'll get onto the police and the landowner's association. [*Puts down the telephone and dials a number*] Hullo, I want to speak to Don Federico. Okay. Hullo, Federico. It's happened. I've just been occupied. I knew they were coming. Some of them even work on my estate. Can't your people do anything? Yes, please do. Send them over quickly. Good. Damned communists. Yes, I'm going to ring the local police now. Thank you. [*Hangs up and dials another number*] Hullo, it's Samuel Benítez, of the Viñas estate. Yes, the landowner. I want to speak to Ramiro Rojas. Alright. [*Pause*] Ramiro, my land is being occupied. They have no authorization or anything. What! Yes, I know all about the Agrarian Reform Law, but the fact is that these peasants are acting off their own bat. You are the force of law and order. You send some of your men over and get them off my land. What? I was lucky not to have lost my land some time ago, under Frei? Are you defending them? What? It's too dangerous? You've stopped doing your job as well, eh? I bet some of you even support the communists. You ate out of my hand before, didn't you? Don Samuel this, Don Samuel that. I know the political situation has changed. But you do your job or I'll get you sacked. I've already contacted Don Federico. What? He cuts no ice now? Here, in San Fernando? We'll see about that. Damn you. [*Hangs up*]

Scene 3 *Three weeks later, on the occupied estate. Peasants are cultivating the fields. Their shacks can be* *seen in the distance. A Chilean flag is flying over a hut, which acts as the office of the peasant leader. Movements from inside the big house can be seen through its windows.*

PEASANT LEADER [*to a group of peasants outside his 'office'*] Friends, we've been here for three weeks and I have some very good news. The 'intervenor' the government promised to send has finally arrived to get Don Samuel to comply with the law and hand over his land. I told you they would back us. This is Mr. Gerardo González. [*The intervenor shakes hands with all the peasants.*]

INTERVENOR Yes, my friends, it's a very clear case. As you know, these big landowners should have been forced out under Frei. What People's Unity is doing is only implementing laws that were not enforced. This estate is way over 200 acres. But you can't have it all. The former landowner has a right to keep some. And he gets government compensation, also. We try to be fair. I'm going to speak to him now and deliver our verdict. I have all the paperwork here. [*Holds up a leather brief-case*]

PEASANT LEADER Friends, we need volunteers in case Don Samuel gets violent. You know that other landowners are in the house to support him, with their men. Quite a few of them are armed. Some of the workers from the towns who arrived the other day will bolster our ranks. Although we're not armed, the other side will be outnumbered. You see the police have not appeared at all. It wasn't like that in the old days, now was it?

LITTLE PEASANT No, they would come and haul you off the estate just for getting a little bit sozzled when you felt like it.

ANOTHER PEASANT When they gave us wine and brandy at *fiesta* times, they didn't mind us getting drunk.

INTERVENOR They wanted you drunk and incapable. That's what the old landowners did in Russia, before the Revolution. Those times are past for us now. You are the ones with the law on your side. And President Allende has sworn to carry out the laws, but never go outside them. So you have to be disciplined. I don't want the landowner manhandled. Our road to socialism is peaceful, remember.

THIRD PEASANT I don't know about socialism, I want land to feed my family and give us security.

INTERVENOR We'll talk about that later. For the moment, we're going to turn this estate into an Agrarian Reform Centre. You'll get a bit of land for your families, but we want to start off as a collective and see how things go. You yourselves are going to be the ones to make the decisions as to what to produce, and how. We're setting up a peasant council for this. But there is one thing you have to do for the government and your fellow Chileans. You must produce more. We need to feed the workers in the towns and cities better. They are helping you here, so you must do something for them.

SECOND PEASANT So what's going to happen after the big boss goes? What's all this about a collective? I work hard, but a lot of the peasants I know hardly work at all.

INTERVENOR You will work as a collective, with individual plots for your families, as I said. All the profits you make will be divided up amongst yourselves, but fifteen per cent will be set aside for re-investment in the estate, your health care, and education. What we call the social fund. Do you understand?

LITTLE PEASANT Well, it'll certainly be better than before.

PEASANT LEADER So, lads, let's have volunteers to escort Mr. González to talk to Don Samuel. [*Ten peasants raise their hands, plus five town workers.*] Good, let's do it. Remember, we're the strong ones now. Don't let them provoke you. They won't dare to shoot. Leave your hoes and spades outside. Remember, 'loaded

33

down with iron, loaded down with fear'. Are you ready?

VOLUNTEERS Ready.

[*González, the intervenor, surrounded by these men, goes up to the front door of the big house and knocks. A maid answers the door.*]

INTERVENOR I've come to speak to the landowner, Mr. Samuel Benítez. I'm a government agrarian reform official. My name is González. [*The maid goes back into the house. The landowner appears at the door. Behind him is a crowd of other men, some with shotguns and pistols in their belts.*]

LANDOWNER I heard who you are and what you've come for: to steal my land and hand it over to this rabble.

INTERVENOR The fact that they're poor doesn't make them a rabble. And if they appear like a rabble to you, it's because you and people like you kept them poor.

LANDOWNER That's a nice little communist speech.

INTERVENOR Actually, I belong to the Socialist Party.

LANDOWNER Just like the comrade and people's friend Salvador Allende. You're here to grab my land. Do you know how long we have had it in my family?

INTERVENOR   That's beside the point. You are contravening the law. You've had plenty of time to know what your legal situation is. I have papers here from the government expropriating you.

LANDOWNER   I don't want to see your damned papers. The rot started under that idiot Frei, who opened the door for you communists to get in. I know the score, but my friends here are witnesses to how I'm being forced off my own land by you thieves. But you won't be able to get away with it for much longer. The decent people in this country won't stand for it. We have allies, you know, strong people. Scum like you won't be allowed to rule for long. Now, get out of my way. [*He emerges from the doorway, beckoning to his friends to follow him. They are a dozen men, some armed. They go to his garage and get into two large old American cars, which roar off through the open gates. The peasants and workers jeer and hoot as the cars speed off.*]

PEASANT LEADER   Well, lads, it wasn't too difficult, was it? Long live People's Unity! Long live President Allende!

PEASANTS AND WORKERS   Long live Allende!

INTERVENOR   Tonight we shall do what we always

do in these cases. We'll have a party and a ceremony when the new title deeds will be given to you.

PEASANTS AND WORKERS Hooray!

PEASANT LEADER We want everyone to keep sober. This is a very important and solemn occasion.

LITTLE PEASANT So you People's Unity people won't let us peasants enjoy ourselves as we always have. You won't last long like that. I don't care what you say. I'm going to get plastered.

PEASANT LEADER For God's sake, *Ratón*, act responsible for once. You don't want the landowner back, do you?

LITTLE PEASANT No. But we're Chilean peasants and we like to have a drink.

PEASANT LEADER Okay, okay. But if you want to better your lives, you'll have to cut down on that and really work. You want more money in your pocket, don't you?

SECOND PEASANT Of course he does, he's just acting the clown, aren't you, *Ratón*?

LITTLE PEASANT Long live Allende!

CURTAIN

ACT 2

Scene 1 *October 1972. Middle and upper-class women, some in fur coats, are banging empty pots and pans in a demonstration in Santiago. Cars, men, and women with loud-hailers. Some working people looking on. The lorry owners, who provide most of the transport for goods in Chile, have struck against the government.*

LARGE WOMAN [*through a loud-hailer*] We want an end to this government of communists, which is destroying Chile. Why do we have to get so many things on the black market? Like meat, sugar, flour, butter, rice, and potatoes. We can't even get underwear at proper prices. [*Sniggers from crowd*]

WORKING-CLASS WOMAN [*shouts from the edge of the demo*] When did you ever use underwear, you old whore?

LARGE WOMAN Cigarettes, razor blades, toilet paper, toothpaste. Where are they?

WORKING-CLASS WOMAN [*to another next to her*] At least she can afford to get them on the black market. [*Loudly*] And who created the black market? Who were the people who cut down production or closed their

factories when the government raised workers' wages?
The rich.

WOMAN IN FUR COAT Why is Allende handing
over our businesses to the rabble? Why can't we get
market prices for our goods? It's communism.

[*Shouts from the well-off crowd: 'El que no salte es un
comunista.' The prosperous citizens jump up and down.*]

WORKING-CLASS WOMAN Serve them right. It's
illegal to cut down production or close factories, just
because they're not making the profits they were.

WOMAN IN FUR COAT Out with the communists!
The country is being ruined. Who invited Fidel Castro
here last year? They want to turn Chile into Cuba. Do
you want to live like the Cubans? With nothing to eat and
no freedom of expression?

[*Chanting from well-off crowd: 'Allende, Allende, la
patria no se vende.'*]

MAN WITH LOUD-HAILER Support the lorry-
owners in their strike!

WORKING-CLASS WOMAN Those bastards are part
of the reason why there are shortages. They've stopped
the food coming in from the countryside. They're trying

to create chaos to bring People's Unity down.

MAN WITH LOUD-HAILER They want to nationalize all private businesses. First they said it was the monopolies only, but their aim is communism. Poverty for everyone and the rabble in control. Allende is a traitor.

SECOND WORKING-CLASS WOMAN Why did the lorry-owners go on strike?

WORKING-CLASS WOMAN The government wanted to set up a nationalized transport system in Aisén, down south. There's hardly any transport at all there, so people can't move around, unless they have a car. Also, the shortages mean the lorry-owners can't get spare parts for the lorries, so they're losing business.

MAN WITH LOUD-HAILER We are asking all respectable people to support this strike. We'll show the scum it's not only they that can strike. Doctors, dentists, accountants, engineers, bank officials, pharmacists, shopkeepers, small manufacturers, anybody who is being ruined by these thieves in power, we want you all to come out.

SECOND WORKING-CLASS WOMAN I've never heard Allende called a thief before. He's not a thief, is he?

WORKING-CLASS WOMAN No, he's not. He's totally honest. Wouldn't take a penny from anybody. His grandfather was the same. Gave all his money away. It's only these rich liars who have the cheek to say that. We've been better off since he came to power. The children all get free milk. Wages have gone up, and that's what the rich can't stand.

SECOND WORKING-CLASS WOMAN I don't think it's right to take over businesses.

WORKING-CLASS WOMAN Well, if they're deliberately being run down, somebody has to step in. And it's quite legal. Allende has sworn never to go outside the Constitution. Sometimes the government has actually stopped businesses being taken over, when the workers got too excited.

SECOND WORKING-CLASS WOMAN But you can't deny there are shortages.

WORKING-CLASS WOMAN The rich are hoarding stuff, sitting on it when they can't get the right prices. And the '*momios*' don't like the government providing the working class with essentials at controlled prices. What do they call those things? Committees for Supplies and Prices. We need them. We haven't got the money to go on the black market. The Americans are squeezing the economy, too.

WOMAN IN FUR COAT [*with loud-hailer*] We are warning them. Remember Jakarta. We will not put up with this forever. There are people in our armed forces that are against this government.

[*Cries of 'Jakarta, Jakarta' and 'Patria y Libertad', 'Allende, Allende, la patria no se vende.'*]

MAN WITH LOUD-HAILER Be quite clear about it. The respectable people have no future under this government. The rabble are taking over, with the help of the Marxists. They're now talking about 'industrial belts' run by the workers. We're going to end up like Russia, where everyone is poor except the commissars.

[*Again, chants of 'Allende, Allende, la patria no se vende.'*]

WORKING-CLASS WOMAN [*to her friend*] Okay, let's go. They're getting excited. You see that crowd of young men there with sticks, the ones in the white cloaks? 'Fatherland and Freedom'. Fascists. They'll use the cudgels on us if they think we're against them.

[*The two slip away.*]

Scene 2 *Barrio Alto, Santiago, June 26, 1973. General Carlos Prats, on his way to work in a chauffeur-driven*

*car, is blocked in a traffic jam. A mob of well-dressed
people start to insult him.*

FUR-COATED WOMAN Prats, you're a disgrace to
the military. You're Allende's poodle. The country's going
to ruin. There are shortages of everything. Why can my
husband only get cigarettes twice a week? Why does my
maid have to take an empty bottle when we need wine?
Why are you propping up these communists?

WELL-DRESSED YOUNG MAN You're not one of
us, even though you live in this neighbourhood. Go and
live in a shantytown. You'd be more at home there, among
the riff-raff.

FUR-COATED WOMAN My husband's business is
going bankrupt, with all those damned price controls.
Allende's wrecking everything. Do you want everybody
in Chile to be poor, like they are in Cuba? Decent people
can't live here any more.

[*Another car bumps into the back of Prats' car.*]

WOMAN LOOKING LIKE A MAN [*hammering on
the windows of Prats' car and making vulgar gestures at
its occupant*] Prats, you should resign from the Army. We
don't want faggots like you. Make way for the real
generals. You'll go the way of that other faggot
Schneider. Our boys took care of him.

PRATS [*winding down his car windows and drawing his revolver*] You insult the Commander-in-Chief of the Chilean Army and you'll get a bullet in you.

MIDDLE-AGED MAN Oh, God, he's drawn his revolver on a woman! [*Other men surround the car and threaten Prats.*] You saw what he did to Virginia? Drew his gun on her.

PRATS [*shouting out of the car window*] I took her for a man. Whoever it is, you'd better show me respect.

WOMAN LOOKING LIKE A MAN Allende faggot. Get out of the Army before they kick you out. [*She and others hammer on the car. Prats gets out of the car, pistol in hand. The mob backs off a little.*]

PRATS [*to his chauffeur*] Alfredo. Get out. Go and get me a taxi, quickly. [*The army chauffeur runs off down a side street. The mob continues to insult Prats, although they are careful not to come too close to him. His chauffeur appears, with a taxi behind. Prats gets into the taxi, followed by the chauffeur. The taxi manages to pull away from the scene, despite attempts by the upper-class mob to block it. The mob attack Prats' car, opening its doors and vandalizing it. Finally they turn it over and set it on fire.*]

Scene 3 *The morning of June 29, 1973. A crowd of people has collected in one corner of the square where La Moneda, the Presidential Palace, is situated. They are looking towards three large tanks, parked in front of the building. From time to time a tank revs its motor and points its gun barrel in another direction, as if to cover itself from different angles.*

WORKING-CLASS MAN   What the hell is that tank doing? Is it attacking La Moneda or defending it?

MAN IN DARK BLUE OVERCOAT   [*he has sleek black hair and olive skin*] It's all over for Allende. The military have finally decided to get rid of the Marxists.

WORKING-CLASS MAN   I think those tanks are defending Allende. The military are still on his side. There's been a revolt somewhere in Santiago, and the tanks are protecting the Palace.

[*A rumbling noise as the turret of one tank turns and points its huge gun at the spectators. A loud-hailer can be heard: 'Keep away from the square! Don't come any closer or you'll be fired upon! Keep your distance!'*]

SMALL MAN   [*looking like an office-clerk*] It's the first time I've seen the military in action. My kids will be thrilled when I tell them.

[*Shots are heard. Sharpshooters are firing sporadically at the tanks from surrounding buildings. A machine-gunner emerges from the turret of one of the tanks and mans his machine gun. The loud-hailer again warns people about approaching the tanks. Further down the street, away from the square, a man is opening his newspaper stand.*]

WORKING-CLASS MAN   Nothing like this has ever happened in Chile.

BLUE-COATED MAN   It's about time it happened. The Tacna regiment will be arriving soon, and then it will be all over.

SMALL MAN   You mean the one that supported Viaux when he tried a coup against Frei?

BLUE-COATED MAN   That's right. Allende's not going to last long.

[*More shots from sharpshooters in the buildings above the crowd. The tank with the machine-gunner moves, repositioning itself so as to point its big gun down the road behind the group of spectators. It stops. The machine-gunner fires several bursts, which take chips of stone from the buildings on the street. The crowd ducks. Some people even lie down. A man buying a newspaper at the stall falls to the ground. He has been hit in the head, and encephalic mass oozes from his wound.*]

WORKING-CLASS MAN   The bastards! They're killing people. What the hell's going on? Allende's troops wouldn't kill civilians.

BLUE-COATED MAN   Don't worry, it'll all be over soon. It's Jakarta.

WORKING-CLASS MAN   What?

BLUE-COATED MAN   Jakarta. Indonesia, a few years ago. The Communist Party there tried to stage a coup, but the military snuffed it out very efficiently. They took millions of prisoners. Indonesia's a big country. Allende here has his own plan for an internal coup to give him supreme power. It looks like our military are nipping it in the bud now.

[*More firing down the same street by the machine-gunner on the tank. A camera crew arrives from a side street and a man starts filming. He starts to walk in the direction of the tank, still filming. The loud-hailer warns: 'Stop advancing, or you'll be shot!' The cameraman stops, then continues moving towards the tank. The machine-gunner fires on him and he and his camera fall to the ground. The machine-gunner fires another burst down the same street as before. Three people fall from the bullets.*]

SMALL MAN   Look over there. [*Pointing to the side of the square on the other side of the tank*] More military. [*Some armoured cars, smaller than the tanks, can be seen approaching slowly in file, towards the tanks. Foot soldiers can be seen in their vicinity.*]

WORKING-CLASS MAN   [*to the man in the dark blue coat*] Are they the Tacna regiment? [*The armoured cars station themselves some fifty yards from the big tank in front of La Moneda. Shouting can be heard from loud-hailers, but the words cannot be distinguished. The newly arrived military seem to be addressing the other.*]

BLUE-COATED MAN   [*disappointed*] No, they're not the Tacna boys.

[*Near the armoured cars more soldiers emerge, positioning themselves on the ground in firing positions, towards the big tanks. More noise from loud-hailers. Then silence for a minute, while nothing happens. Then the soldiers from the armoured cars fire on the tanks. People start shooting again from the windows of the surrounding buildings. The large tanks rev up their motors, the machine-gunner disappears inside the turret of his tank and it moves off towards the street at whose corner the spectators had positioned themselves. They flatten themselves to the walls of the buildings on either side of the street as the tank roars off, past the newspaper stall, where someone has placed newspapers over the dead bodies lying in the street. As the tank roars off up the street, the tank commander's head can be seen, in a wine-red beret, turning agitatedly this way and that. The other two tanks rush up the street after it.*]

SMALL MAN Those tanks must have been attacking the Palace, trying to get Allende to step down. And those armoured cars must be from a loyal regiment.

[*Loud-hailer from the armoured cars: 'Please disperse! The situation is dangerous here. You cannot help the government by hanging around here. Tune into your radios at home. President Allende is going to make a speech to explain the situation. Move off peacefully, please.' A soldier places a military overcoat on the body of the dead cameraman. 'Please disperse! The government has everything under control.'*]

Scene 4 *The same evening (June 29). The square of La Moneda, whose balcony is illuminated. Large crowds of workers are listening to the speeches of President Allende, representatives of the People's Unity coalition, and trade union leaders.*

CROWD *¡Allende, Allende, el pueblo te defiende! ¡El pueblo, unido, jamás será vencido!* Dismiss Congress! Power to the people!

ALLENDE It is heartening to see you all here, supporting the people's government after the incidents of this morning, when one regiment rose up futilely to try to topple the people from power. Make no mistake, those rebels will be given the punishment they deserve. They were only a small fraction of our Armed Forces, which remained overwhelmingly loyal. General Prats, the Commander-in-Chief of the Army, personally disarmed some of the rebel commanders. The Armed Forces of Chile are still behind this government, in accordance with their constitutional duty. I ask you to keep faith with them.

SMALL MAN I didn't see Prats in the square.

WORKER No, he was on the other side of La Moneda. There were three tanks surrounding the Defence Ministry on the *Alameda*. Those were the ones he dealt with.

CROWD *¡Soldado, amigo, el pueblo está contigo!* Arms to the people! Power to the people!

ALLENDE We have to create People's Power. But it cannot be antagonistic to or independent of the government, which is the fundamental force and platform for the workers to advance in the revolutionary process.

CROWD Drive the Yankees out of Chile, now!

ALLENDE We said we would carry out the program of the People's Unity and push the process forward within constitutional and legal channels, and this is what we shall do. I am not going to close Congress. [*Boos and whistles from the crowd*] If necessary, I shall call on the people, in accordance with the powers invested in me legally and constitutionally, to pronounce its judgement in a referendum on our government's policies. In the meantime, I want the people of Chile to go back to work and continue to create the wealth that Chile needs for giving you a better life. We know that the main civilian leaders of the coup have taken refuge in a foreign embassy.

VOICES IN THE CROWD Death to Pablo Rodríguez and Benjamín Matte! Death to Jarpa and Hasbún! Death to Vilarín! *¡Paredón! ¡El que no salte es un momio!* [*The crowd jumps up and down.*]

ALLENDE And now, comrades, I must ask you all to disperse peacefully and continue working for the revolutionary process. Thank you.

CROWD *¡Allende, Allende, el pueblo te defiende! ¡El pueblo, unido, jamás será vencido! ¡Soldado, amigo, el pueblo está contigo!*

[*A group of people turn to go home, trailing their banners behind them.*]

YOUNG WORKER   So what's Allende going to do? I'm not very clear. Is he really going to punish those tank commanders?

ANOTHER WORKER   I should damn well hope so. They should be shot. Why doesn't he shut Congress down if the Armed Forces are still on his side? Those bastards are blocking all our programs for social reform.

WORKING-CLASS WOMAN   I don't think he can. And anyway, you heard what he said. The People's Unity government has to abide by the rules of the Constitution and stick by the pact they made with the Christian Democrats before Allende was sworn in. Those are the rules of the game, and we should stick together and support him.

SECOND WORKER   But will the opposition abide by those rules? I'm sure Frei and Aylwin won't, and they are the ones who really wield the power inside the Christian Democrat Party. The Christian Democrats are supporting this new lorry-owners' strike. Tomic, Leighton, and Fuentealba have lost control. I think Chicho is not very sure about what to do. He needs to assert his authority and purge the Army. He's a good man and will never betray the people, but I think he has to come down heavy.

YOUNG WORKER   You're right. But it's a dicey situation. And I don't think People's Unity government agrees about what it should do. All those people calling for the 'armed struggle' may be right. But how will they get it off the ground? And who has got arms? The Armed Forces will never allow a parallel military power to exist alongside their own.

WOMAN But it was heartening to see how many people turned out this evening. Didn't they say there were twenty thousand? This government is really popular with the working class. And many factories were occupied by their workers when the news of the uprising came through. [*The group leaves the stage. Others are singing 'El arado', made famous by Víctor Jara.*]

Scene 5 *The official residence of President Allende, on Tomás Moro Street in the high-class area of Santiago. August 22, 1973. Late at night. Allende, his secretary Miriam Contreras, Generals Pinochet, Brady, Sepúlveda, Pickering, Urbina, González, etc. President Allende is in his sixties, neatly dressed and wearing spectacles. His manner is courteous and firm. Pinochet is a few years younger, heavy-jowled, with slicked-back graying hair and a folksy, ingratiating manner.*

ALLENDE Generals, you know why you have been asked to dinner here tonight. We have a very serious matter to discuss concerning General Carlos Prats, the Commander-in-Chief of the Army. For some months there has been a vicious campaign against this loyal and patriotic military servant of Chile. It started with the disgraceful incident of June 26 in the *Barrio Alto* when he was insulted and missed being lynched by the skin of his teeth. I don't need to tell you who was behind this incident. We have evidence that it was cooked up by Fatherland and Freedom, our local fascists. A radio station later gave a broadcast of the incident and called General Prats 'a coward', someone who should not be the head of our Armed Forces. The next day, *El Mercurio* called for a military government. And two days later, as you know, there was an attempted coup, which was defeated with the help of many of you here present. You saw General Prats' courage in putting down that coup when he personally disarmed some of the tank commanders, and I know you must be concerned at this campaign to damage his reputation. Yesterday there was a demonstration of women outside the General's home, including the wives of six other generals and other high-ranking officers, calling on him to step down as Commander-in-Chief of the Army and let other generals forge our country's military power. Later on, General Bonilla visited him at his home when he was sick in bed to ask him to resign (and I quote) 'in the name of the corps of generals because you are a disgrace to our institution, in your excessive loyalty to Allende's government.' To cap it all, Bonilla went on to say: 'We have taken all necessary steps to cleanse the honour of our Armed Forces, once and for all.' I had this from the mouth of General Prats himself when I went to see him after Bonilla left. He warned me that a coup was being prepared. Now you are the generals closest to General Prats. I want to hear what you have to say and how we are to deal with this situation.

PINOCHET My respect and friendship for General Prats are not something recent. They are longstanding facts, and there are no limits. And just as deep and strong is my loyalty to the President, and my need to affirm the constitutional function of the Armed Forces.

GONZÁLEZ General Prats is tired. He needs to be replaced. He cannot possibly carry on.

BRADY There is no question of General Prats' resigning. He must stay on to maintain discipline in the Armed Forces and avoid civil war.

SEPÚLVEDA I protest at the insults to General Prats. The Army's reaction to this was disgraceful. I can no longer remain in such an institution. Tomorrow I shall hand in my resignation.

PINOCHET I must repeat my protest at the abuse heaped on my colleague, General Prats.

PICKERING I feel unwell. Someone help me onto the sofa. [*He is lifted onto a sofa.*]

ALLENDE Please excuse me. I have to make a phone call. [*Goes to his private office. To his secretary*] Miriam, please call up all the People's Unity party leaders and the head of the Trade Union Federation. Tell them that, given the seriousness of the military situation, I have decided to dismiss some generals we know are involved in a coup plot. They are Generals Bonilla, Arellano Stark, Baeza, Forestier, Palacios Ruhman, and Benavides. I am going to discuss with the army high command a plan to defend the government by collaboration between the regular forces and trade unions. I am sending General Pinochet to coordinate. He is to report back here later. [*Pinochet leaves.*]

Scene 6 *La Moneda, August 23. Allende, Generals Prats and Pinochet, and Allende's young Spanish political adviser Joan Garcés.*

PRATS Mr. President, I am handing in my resignation. You know all the strain I have been under, particularly in these last few months. I am exhausted, and the last straw came when I asked my corps of generals to endorse a declaration of protest at the harm done to my person and rank by the women's march and demonstration in front of my house. There were twenty-two generals present, and out of these eighteen refused to back my declaration. My only supporters were Pinochet, Brady, Sepúlveda, and Pickering. I feel I no longer have authority with the

Armed Forces to restrain the coup that is undoubtedly being plotted.

ALLENDE This is very bad news, General. You have always had my complete confidence and the government cannot afford to lose a man like you, especially in his capacity as head of the Army. But I know your problems. General Pinochet, you are the army second-in-command. What do you advise?

PINOCHET Mr. President. I think you have no alternative. General Prats' situation has become impossible.

JOAN GARCÉS Mr. President, accepting General Prats' resignation is most unwise. He has been under great strain, as we all know, but he is indispensable to your government.

ALLENDE General Prats has lost control of the Army. Also, he is not emotionally in a condition to do his duty. I see no alternative to accepting his resignation.

PRATS Mr. President, I do not want to run the risk of dividing the Armed Forces of Chile. My departure will make it easier to maintain their unity around the government. General Pinochet can take over from me. He is my second-in-command, and also the surest general for maintaining army discipline.

ALLENDE I need time to think this thing over. Write me an official letter.

PRATS I shall do that. Do I have your permission to make it public?

ALLENDE You do. I have always had the maximum confidence in you, as you know, General.

CURTAIN

ACT 3

Scene 1 *Defence Minister Orlando Letelier's office. 10 a.m., Monday, September 10. Letelier is an elegantly-dressed, handsome, dandyish, and sophisticated sort of man. He is awaiting the arrival of General Pinochet, whom President Allende has appointed as the new Commander-in-Chief of the Army.*

AIDE General Pinochet is here, sir.

LETELIER Show him in please.

PINOCHET Good morning, Minister.

LETELIER Good morning, General. I hope you bring good news with your briefing.

PINOCHET I do. The military situation seems to be quieter. I have been in contact with various units and everything seems under control. I met with President Allende yesterday and I was rather worried then, but things seemed to have settled down.

LETELIER I hope so. What else is there?

PINOCHET Preparations for the usual military

Independence Day parade are going ahead as normal.

LETELIER [*drily*] Maybe that's the reason why there seems more movement than usual.

PINOCHET As a former graduate of the Military Academy, you will understand, sir.

LETELIER Yes.

PINOCHET Also, tomorrow I shall give you a memorandum on the material that the Armed Forces could acquire in the United States and the Soviet Union. To be quite frank, our commanders are not enthusiastic about the material the Soviets have on offer, but they will accept it. I myself favour buying from a diversity of sources.

LETELIER Good.

PINOCHET However, our commanders are against Soviet officers coming to Chile to train military personnel. They think it would be better if our people went to the Soviet Union, just as they go to the United States.

LETELIER I see. Anything else?

PINOCHET Oh, yes. The preparations to try Major

Roberto Souper are being speeded up.

LETELIER I should think so. It's more than two months now that he led that tank regiment against the government. They killed a dozen people.

PINOCHET Yes, sir. Also we're getting on with the indictment of the two officers who insulted General Prats on August 21.

LETELIER Good. Carry on. The President told me what General Bonilla said. Accusing General Prats of excessive loyalty to Allende's government. What gall. The Chilean Armed Forces have sworn to respect the constitutionally elected government, and when the Army Commander upholds his constitutional oath, he is insulted. And with General Prats sick in bed, too.

PINOCHET I am personally going to ask Generals Bonilla and Arellano Stark to request their retirement to the Army Reserve.

LETELIER Please do so. Regard it as an urgent matter. Is that all?

PINOCHET Yes, sir.

LETELIER Good, General. I shall see you out. I am leaving too, to give a lecture here in the Ministry on the

People's Unity strategy and the Armed Forces.

PINOCHET So I heard, sir. Allow me to help you on
with your coat. I shall accompany you a short way. Would
you like me to carry your briefcase?

LETELIER That is kind of you, General. I have so
many papers here.

[*They leave.*]

Scene 2 *President Allende's official residence, Tomás
Moro Street. September 11, 1973, 6:30 a.m. The main
living room. Pictures by left-wing painters on the wall:
Picasso, Siqueiros, Miró, Portocarrero, Guayasamín, and
Matta. Photographs of Ho Chi Minh, Che Guevara, and
Arturo Alessandri Palma, the restorer of the Chilean
parliamentary regime in 1925. Allende comes in dressed
in a magenta turtle-neck sweater and dark-grey trousers.
In the breast pocket of his tweed jacket is a red silk
handkerchief. He is followed by an aide. The phone rings.
The aide picks it up. Letelier, Augusto Olivares (Allende's
press secretary), and Joan Garcés arrive.*

AIDE It's serious, sir.

ALLENDE Give me the phone. [*Speaks into it*] Yes,
yes, I'm listening. Thank you. [*Puts down the phone.*

Other members of Allende's staff have come silently into the room.] My friends, the Navy has risen up in Valparaíso. The officers of a submarine and a cruiser. Six lorry-loads of marines were intercepted on the Valparaíso-Santiago road by the *Carabineros*. The Navy, damn their eyes. I knew it would be them. [*Picks up the phone again and rings several numbers, without reply. Finally, he gets through.*] General Brady, the Navy has rebelled in Valparaíso. Take measures to put them down. What? If you're not going to do it, be a man and say so. The Army is in control in Valparaíso? That's not what I heard. Okay. [*Hangs up*] It seems the Army's loyal. [*Picks up the phone*] The President of the Republic speaking. I want to talk to General Pinochet. He's not at home? Thank you. [*Hangs up, rings another number, but receives no reply*]

LETELIER I've just rung my office at the Ministry of Defence, sir. Admiral Carvajal replied. What was he doing there? He said there were no troops in Santiago, or if there were, it was just for an arms search. He was humming and hawing and stuttering. He said they were trying to contact Valparaíso. It's very fishy, sir.

ALLENDE Orlando, you need to go immediately to your ministry to see what's going on.

LETELIER Yes, sir. [*He leaves.*]

AUGUSTO OLIVARES Mr. President, do you want me to ring General Prats?

ALLENDE [*resignedly*] No, Augusto. [*He sighs.*] It's better we don't speak to him. He can't do much good now. Try to get Admiral Montero on the phone. We'll send him to Valparaíso.

OLIVARES [*rings*] No use, sir. No reply.

GARCÉS Mr. President, I feel the whole thing is under way. We must silence the opposition radios at once.

ALLENDE You're right, Juan Enrique. [*To the aide*] Give orders for Radios Agricultura and Minería to be shut down by emergency presidential decree. And *El Mercurio* too. [*The aide leaves.*]

OLIVARES [*from a phone*] The Air Force is going into the industrial *cordones* right now on an arms raid.

ALLENDE Bastards, intimidating and brutalising everybody when they know nobody has any weapons. It's civil war. The Army and *Carabineros* are on our side. The Navy and Air Force are against us. I must go to La Moneda immediately. [*To the aide*] Phone the *Carabineros* to send troops there. [*All exit.*]

Scene 3 *La Moneda Presidential Palace. 7:30 a.m., the same morning.*

AIDE [*at a phone*] Mr. President, I've just got through to the commander of the Second Army division. He says the Army is loyal. This is confirmed by the commander of the Santiago garrison. [*Rings again*] I can confirm that the *Carabineros* are with us. General Sepúlveda Galindo says he is mobilizing against the insurrection.

ALLENDE Thank God for that. Those are *Carabinero* tanks outside. Good protection.

[*A group of young men dressed in dark suits and holding sub-machine guns enters. It is the presidential body guard. Its leader addresses Allende.*]

LEADER We're ready for combat, sir.

ALLENDE [*at phone*] Good, lads. [*Rings repeatedly*] None of the top commanders are answering the phone. I'll bet they're all in on the plot. I'm going to have to make a speech over the radio. [*He telephones.*] Hullo, Radio Corporación, this is President Allende. I need to broadcast a speech to the people immediately. Can you get me on the air? Thank you, I knew you would. [*Starts speech over the phone*] 'People and workers of Chile, this is President Allende speaking. Valparaíso has been occupied by rebel armed forces and the government asks

65

for your help. The workers are to occupy their work posts and keep calm. Santiago is normal. I myself shall stay in La Moneda and defend the people's government.
Workers, be on your guard and avoid provocations. Your government is awaiting the response of the loyal armed forces to the uprising. They know that I, as President, will do my duty. Workers! Await your orders from the President.' [*Puts down the phone*]

GARCÉS Mr. President. The workers cannot simply wait to see what happens. They should act. We should have prepared them for this long ago. May I call Calderón at the Trade Union Confederation?

ALLENDE Yes, call him. [*Garcés phones Calderón, the Trade Union vice-president. He hands the phone over to Allende.*] Rolando, we have an attempted coup on our hands. You must get your people to shut down the opposition radio stations. Radio Agricultura and Radio Minería. Occupy *El Mercurio* as well. You'll need troop support? Of course, I'll try to arrange it. Good luck. [*Puts the phone down*]

GARCÉS What about General Prats?

ALLENDE Don't worry about Prats. He's in a safe house.

GARCÉS I'm worried about Letelier. Where is he? You

know General Prats told us last week that there was a plot to assassinate him.

ALLENDE   [*to a member of his personal escort*] Go to the Ministry of Defence and find Letelier. [*The man leaves and Allende goes into conference with his aides for a few minutes. This is interrupted when a man dressed in civilian clothes comes in through the door. It is Colonel Valenzuela, Allende's Under-Secretary for War.*]

VALENZUELA   Mr. President, I have just been to the Ministry of Defence and they would not let me in. It's been occupied by the Army. Minister Letelier went there before me and was taken prisoner by his own military guard. [*Dismay on the faces of all*]

ALLENDE   So it's that bad. I need to make another speech over the radio. [*An aide goes off to a corner phone, makes contact, and then hands over the phone to Allende. The latter can be seen but not heard talking into the phone. Another phone rings. Garcés picks it up.*]

GARCÉS   Yes, Major Sánchez, he's here, but he's making a speech over the radio. You'll have to wait to speak to him. What news do you have? Hullo, I asked you for your news. [*Turning to Olivares*] He's not replying. [*Allende has finished his speech over the radio and comes over to the other phone.*]

ALLENDE Yes, Major Sánchez, I'm listening. What? Tell General Van Schowen that the President of Chile does not flee the country by plane. Tell him to behave like a soldier. As for me, I know how to do my duty as the President of the Republic. Major Sánchez, you are to come immediately to La Moneda. [*Rings off. To the group of advisers*] The Air Force Chief of Staff is offering me a plane to leave the country. He ordered Sánchez to go to the Ministry of Defence and call here because he didn't dare make the proposition personally. Do they really think I'm going to run away? I remember being with President Aguirre Cerda in 1939 when a similar situation arose. General Ariosto Herrera had risen up in Santiago and sent the President's Air Force aide over to La Moneda to offer the President a plane for leaving the country. Old Aguirre Cerda was in a chair smoking a cigarette and he refused. He said: 'Look here, Major, I have all my life been a man of law and order. And now I am the President of the Republic. They will have to come and get me here because I am not leaving.' Herrera never appeared.

GARCÉS Yes, Mr. President, but Herrera did not have the Pentagon, Nixon, and Henry Kissinger behind him. His attempted coup was a purely Chilean affair.

ALLENDE That's true. But we still may have a section of the Armed Forces on our side.

GARCÉS I know the high command of *Carabineros* will support us. We should have created structures long ago for the workers to liaise with the *Carabineros* in the event of what's happening now. It would have made us much stronger in Santiago.

ALLENDE I know, Juan Enrique. It was your idea and we should have implemented it. It was a big mistake not to. But, as you know, not all the parties in our coalition were in favour. But let's be optimistic. Those *Carabinero* troops and tanks outside look pretty solid. [*Enter General Sepúlveda Galindo, the Commander-in-Chief of Carabineros*] Hullo, General, what news do you have?

SEPÚLVEDA GALINDO There's some confusion, Mr. President. I need to call General Parada. [*Allende motions him over to a phone. Sepúlveda Galindo raises his voice.*] General Parada, the *Carabineros* have always stood by the elected government. I am the Director General. You are only the Prefect-in-Chief of *Carabineros* in Santiago. You only take orders from me. [*Allende listens and finally picks up another phone.*]

ALLENDE Víctor, please get General Prats to come to La Moneda. [*Garcés fiddles with the knobs of a radio.*]

GARCÉS Radio Agricultura. [*A military march is heard, then another, then another.*] Listen, sir. We haven't been able to put it out of action. [*The military music* *stops and a voice is heard. Allende and his advisers listen attentively. Garcés turns up the sound.*]

RADIO AGRICULTURA 'The President of Chile must proceed immediately to hand over his office to the Armed Forces and *Carabineros* of Chile. The press, radio, and television channels controlled by the parties of the People's Unity coalition must suspend their broadcasts immediately, otherwise they will be attacked by air and land. This order is signed by the Government of the Military Junta of the Chilean Armed Forces and *Carabineros*. For the Army, General Augusto Pinochet; the Navy, Admiral José Toribio Merino; the Air Force, General Gustavo Leigh; the *Carabineros*, General César Mendoza.'

ALLENDE [*quietly*] I'm going to make another broadcast. [*Goes over to a phone in the corner. Fragments of his speech can be heard.*] 'This is a holocaust... I will not hand over my command.' [*Hangs up the phone*] Three traitors, three traitors. [*Drums his fingers on a desk*]

GARCÉS Nobody can be surprised about Leigh. Look at all those brutal raids on factories by his Air Force troops. Admiral Montero must have been forced out by that old bastard Merino. Mendoza's taken charge of the *Carabineros*. And he was always so obsequious to you, sir, almost grovelling. And what about Pinochet? How many times did he swear he would be with the government to the last? And now he must be the leader of the whole thing, as Commander-in-Chief of the Army. Dirty dog. No wonder we couldn't get him on the phone at his home earlier on this morning. I'm wondering about Brady and his troops in Santiago. Has he been toppled or was he lying to us when we spoke to him? I know Prats never trusted him, for all his reputation for being 'the most Marxist' of the military chiefs.

ALLENDE   [*bitterly*] I appointed Leigh and Pinochet myself. Who would have thought Pinochet was in on this? He even rang me up a week ago asking how the heads of the Armed Forces could congratulate me on the third anniversary of my presidential election victory.

GARCÉS   For the first time in the history of the professional army of Chile, its Commander-in-Chief is leading an insurrection against the President of the Republic.

ALLENDE   Exactly. In 1891, when the Navy rose up for Congress and against President Balmaceda, the Army supported the President. Let's try to contact these rebel commanders. [*Colonel Valenzuela goes to a phone and dials. After a time he gets through.*]

VALENZUELA   Hullo, General Pinochet. Colonel Valenzuela. The President is ordering you to come to La

Moneda immediately to explain your position. We must avoid a catastrophe. Hullo, can you hear me? You refuse to come? [*To Allende*] Sir, he has hung up on me.

OLIVARES   Where is General Prats?

[*A noise of engines revving is heard from outside. Allende goes to the window and sticks his head out. After a short time, he starts waving, then comes back.*]

ALLENDE   The people are on our side, as they have always been. I saw about a hundred ordinary folk passing by. When they saw me, they applauded. But the *Carabinero* tanks, buses, and troops are leaving. General Sepúlveda Galindo, can you explain this?

SEPÚLVEDA GALINDO   I don't know, sir. I'll try to find out. [*Leaves the room. After a while he returns.*] The *Carabinero* telephone exchange has been taken over and the *Carabinero* troops are receiving their orders by radio. My high command is isolated.

ALLENDE   Send troops to retake the telecommunications center.

SEPÚLVEDA GALINDO   I have no men, only those attached to the high command, about 200 metres from here.

ALLENDE How many are they?

SEPÚLVEDA GALINDO Fifty, plus officers.

ALLENDE Order them to come here immediately.

GARCÉS [*to Sepúlveda Galindo*] General, the only thing left for us to do is to give arms to the people. Can you do this?

SEPÚLVEDA GALINDO [*in stupefaction*] Me distribute arms? How?

[*The President's three military aides approach Allende. These are Major Jorge Grez (Navy), Lieutenant Colonel Sergio Badiola (Army), and Major Jorge Sánchez (Air Force).*]

GREZ Mr. President, the Armed Forces are asking you to hand over power.

BADIOLA Sir, you have no alternative. You must save your life.

ALLENDE Commanders, if you want you can go back to your institutions. You are free to do so.

[*The noise of jet planes screaming over the palace can be heard. Hernán del Canto, a prominent member of*

Allende's own Socialist Party appears and approaches the President.]

DEL CANTO Mr. President, my party would like to know what you would like us to do.

ALLENDE [*bitterly*] I know which is my place and what *I* have to do. You never asked me for my opinion before. Why are you asking for it now? You, who boasted so much, should know what you have to do. I have known all along what *my* duty was. We've been under a ferocious attack from the right for some time, but our own people are making things even worse. A couple of days ago I got a letter from the People's Unity political committee about the crisis. They said no to everything I proposed as a way out. They wanted no pact with the Christian Democrats, no people's referendum on the government's Social Area policy, no government of national security and defence, and no vote of confidence for me to take unilateral decisions. What did they want? An emperor with no clothes? Corvalán finally came round on the referendum decision and unilateral powers, but that still left me floundering. And you come and ask me what you should do. Now?

GARCÉS Sir, cannot you dismiss these rebel generals? Is there no one to replace them in any garrison? Is there not one loyal regiment?

ALLENDE Not one regiment, Juan Enrique.

GARCÉS So we're completely high and dry. The *Carabineros* were our last chance. No party and no workers' organization is in any condition to do anything, either in isolation or in combination. What our ultra-leftists wanted, 'the destruction of the bourgeois state', has come about. So, when are they going to spring into action? And with what? We're sitting ducks.

ALLENDE I'm going to make another speech before all our communications are shut down. At least we can let the people know we went down fighting. [*Goes to a telephone, dials a number, converses and then makes his speech. An aide tunes in the radio so that everybody can hear.*]

'At this moment planes are flying over the Presidential Palace. Probably they will fill us full of bullets. But let them know that we are here, at least with our example, that in this country there are men who know how to do their duty. I shall do it by the mandate from the people and by the conscious will of a president who has the dignity of his office. In the name of the most sacred interests of the people, in the name of the *patria*, I call upon you to tell them to have faith. History is not brought to a stop by repression or by crime. This is a stage which will be overcome. This is a hard and difficult moment. It is possible that they will crush us. But tomorrow will belong to the people, the workers. Humanity is advancing towards the conquest of a better life. The people must be alert and vigilant. It must not allow itself to be massacred. But it must also defend its conquests. It must defend the right to build with its effort a more worthy and better life.'

GARCÉS [*to Olivares*] What are the People's Unity parties doing now? Are they finally getting together to form a united front or what?

[*Enter Generals Urbina and Álvarez. They look flustered and embarrassed.*]

URBINA We have a message from the General Headquarters of *Carabineros*.

ALLENDE Mendoza must have got you up early.

SEPÚLVEDA GALINDO You must behave like men. You must say what you have to say to the President in person. Not by sending troops. You have to be men in these things.

ALLENDE [*at the phone*] Hullo, Radio Corporación, can you hear me? [*Listens and finally puts down the phone*] Their radio station was bombed. [*Dials another number*] Radio Portales. Hullo. What? The Air Force has bombed you as well? [*Puts down the phone*] We have only one radio station I can broadcast over. [*Picks up the phone*] Radio Magallanes. President Allende. Can you hear me? You're still on the air. Thank goodness. I need to make a speech immediately. I can? Thank you. [*Starts his speech. An aide tunes into Radio Magallanes and everybody listens to Allende's fifth speech over the air.*]

'Fellow-countrymen. This is your President Allende speaking. The Chilean Armed Forces have committed an act of betrayal by rising up today against the legally elected government of your country. They may silence all our radio stations, and I may be taking my leave of you. Perhaps this will be the last opportunity for me to address you. The Air Force has bombed Radio Portales and Radio Corporación. My words do not show bitterness, only disappointment, and they will be the moral punishment of those who have betrayed the oath they took: Chilean soldiers, commanders-in-chief, the self-appointed Admiral Merino, and General Mendoza, a servile general who only yesterday declared his solidarity and loyalty to the government, and who has also proclaimed himself Director General of *Carabineros*.

'Faced with such facts, I can only say to the workers that I am not going to resign. Swept along by a historical crisis, I will pay for my loyalty to the people with my life. And I say to you that I am certain that the seed that we are planting in the true consciousness of thousands and thousands of Chileans cannot be totally destroyed. In the

name of the most sacred interests of the people, in the
name of the *patria*, we call upon you all to keep faith.
History cannot be stopped either by repression or crime.
This is a stage which we shall go beyond. This is a hard
and difficult moment; it is possible that they will crush
us. But tomorrow will belong to the people, to the
workers. Humanity is advancing in its conquest of a
better life. Workers of my *patria*: I want to thank you for
the loyalty that you have always shown, the trust you
deposited in a man who was merely an interpreter of a
great longing for justice, who pledged his word to respect
the Constitution and the law and did precisely that.

'This is the definitive moment, the last at which I can
address you. Listen hard to what I am saying. Foreign
capital, imperialism in alliance with the forces of
reaction, has created the climate for the armed forces to
break with their tradition, that which Schneider affirmed
and Major Araya re-affirmed, victims of the same social
sector that today is at home waiting to conquer by
someone else's hand the power to continue defending its
profits and privileges. I am speaking, above all, to the
lowly woman of our land, to the peasant woman who
believed in us, to the woman factory worker who worked
more, to the mother who heard about our concern for
children. I am speaking to the country's professionals, to
the patriotic professionals, to those that for many days
have been working against the sedition nurtured by the
associations of professionals, class associations for

defending the advantages of a capitalist society.

'I am speaking to young people and to those who sang and gave their joy and fighting spirit, I am speaking to the man of Chile, to the factory worker, to the peasant, to the intellectual, to those who will face persecution, because in our country fascism has been showing its hand for a long time, by destroying bridges, cutting railway lines, and blowing up oil and gas pipe-lines, in the face of the silence of those who should have acted. They shouldered the burdens. History will judge them.

'Shortly Radio Magallanes will be silenced and the quiet sound of my voice will reach you no longer. It does not matter. You will continue to hear me. I will always be by your side. At least you will remember me as a worthy man who was loyal to his country. The people must defend itself, but not sacrifice itself. The people must not let itself be wiped out or be filled full of bullets, but neither must it accept humiliation.

'Workers of my country, I have faith in Chile and in its destiny. Other men will go beyond this grey and bitter moment when treachery is trying to impose itself. You should continue to know that, much earlier than later, the great avenues for free men to walk along in order to build a better society will open up. Long live Chile, long live the people, long live the workers!

'These are my last words, in the certainty that the sacrifice will not be in vain. I am sure that, at least, there will be a moral sanction that will punish felony, cowardice and treachery.' [*Thanks the broadcasters and hangs up the phone. Addressing his three military aides*] Gentlemen, you can leave if you wish. *I* am staying. [*They leave. Noise of Hawker Hunter jets flying over La Moneda. Allende speaks into a phone, then hangs up.*] Two minutes more and we shall be under attack.

[*Gunfire starts and will not finish until the end of the act. A radio announces that orders have been given to bomb La Moneda unless Allende surrenders.*]

ALLENDE There are going to be casualties here, but let's cut them down to a minimum. [*To his Carabinero Presidential Guards*] If you want to leave, you can. [*They leave. Generals Urbina and Álvarez also leave, with no apology.*] General Sepúlveda Galindo, you may also leave.

SEPÚLVEDA GALINDO No sir, I do not want to leave.

ALMEYDA President Allende, the People's Unity ministers present here wish to talk to you in private.

ALLENDE As you wish. [*He leads them to another room. The ministers are Clodomiro Almeyda (Foreign*

*Relations); Carlos Briones (Interior); Jaime Tohá
(Agriculture); José Tohá (ex-Minister of Defence), and
Fernando Flores (General Secretary of Government).
After a couple of minutes, Allende and his ministers
reappear.*]

ALLENDE My place is here, comrades, I am not going
to surrender just to save my life.

SEPÚLVEDA GALINDO I have decided to leave, sir.

ALLENDE Very well, general. [*The phone rings.*]
Hullo, Allende here. Joignant, what has been happening
to your Detective Branch? What? You've resigned? But I
appointed you myself. Your duty is to stay at your post
and carry out my orders. None of our people has yet
betrayed us. Don't you feel ashamed? [*Throws up his
arms in despair*] Hullo, I can't hear properly. There are
other voices coming over the phone wires. What? [*Turns
to his officials*] I can hear General Baeza's voice. He says
he is the commander of operations in Santiago. Listen.
[*Repeats the words he hears*] 'Nobody from the staff of
La Moneda must survive, especially Allende. We have to
exterminate them like cockroaches. The objective is to be
destroyed by land and air!' That's what we're up against,
comrades. How many of us are there here in the Palace?
About 50. Only about 20 of us are armed. We're facing
troops, tanks, and jet planes. What do you want to do, my
friends?

A GROUP OF AIDES [*Arsenio Poupin (General Undersecretary of Government); Augusto Olivares (Press Secretary); Jaime Barrios (economist), Claudio Gimeno (sociologist); four doctors; Jorge Klein (psychiatrist); Eduardo Paredes (ex Director General of Police Detective Branch); Ricardo Pincheira (Secretarial Service of the Socialist Party); Enrique Huerta (Palace Intendant)*] We'll stay, sir.

ALLENDE [*to Garcés*] Juan Enrique, you must leave.

GARCÉS [*surprised*] Why, sir?

ALLENDE In the end, somebody has to tell what happened, and only you can do that. [*To his aides*] Am I not right?

AIDES Yes, sir. [*Garcés shakes hands with Allende and leaves.*]

[*By now smoke and flames are filling La Moneda. The armed survivors put on gas-masks and start shooting at the troops attacking the building. Allende himself is wearing a helmet and carrying a sub-machine gun. The windows are being shattered by fire from tanks. Tear gas, explosions from grenades. After a while the first rebel soldiers enter the first floor of La Moneda, where Allende and his team are. Allende is shot by a captain, in the belly. Another soldier shoots him, also in the belly. It is only then that they realise whom they have shot.*]

CAPTAIN That's him! Allende!

[*More fire. Allende by now is dead, riddled with bullets. But the soldiers are driven back downstairs by Allende's loyal fighters. Dr. Enrique París (a psychiatrist and Allende's personal doctor) takes his pulse and indicates he is dead. An aide appears with a Chilean flag and Dr. París drapes it over Allende's body. The rebel troops return and overcome all the defenders.*]

FINAL CURTAIN

PINOCHET

Peter Turton

*To all those who suffered torture, death,
and imprisonment under Pinochet*

CONTENTS

For the writing of *Pinochet* I should like to acknowledge the help afforded me, in particular, by two books: *Yo, Augusto*, by Ernesto Ekaizer, very informative throughout; and *The Pinochet File*, by Peter Kornbluh, especially for one particular document.

'This tyrant, whose sole name blisters our tongues,
Was once thought honest.'

-Macbeth

ACT 1

Scene 1 *September 11, 1973. The Chilean Presidential Palace is billowing smoke. In a nearby street, troops are battering at the door of a building. They break it down and rush in screaming. Firing is heard within the building. The soldiers emerge, dragging prisoners, beating them with rifle butts and kicking them.*

OFFICER Get them into the wagon. You know where to take them. No, not these four. They're not going anywhere. Line them up against the wall, hands on head. [*Screams*] Hands on head, can't you hear, you Marxist shit? Shooting at us, eh? [*Screams*] Face to the wall. [*The prisoners are manhandled face to the wall.*] Shoot them. [*They are shot.*] Okay, now drive off. [*The wagon rumbles off with the other prisoners.*] Over there, that half-open door. In you go. [*The soldiers smash down the door.*] There's a whole nest of them there. Get them all out.

[*Constant gunfire and explosions. The roar of tanks and armoured cars in the distance. From time to time an armoured car or lorry passes, full of prisoners. Soldiers emerge from the doorway, dragging and beating their captives as before.*]

OFFICER 2 Make them lie down. On their faces. Look

sharp. [*Pulls out his pistol and executes three men, with a bullet in the back of the head*] You other fuckers keep on your faces. [*Kicks them. Machine gun fire is heard.*] Shall I finish them off, captain?

OFFICER   No, take them away. [*The prisoners are made to get up and bundled into a lorry.*] Hold it, there's more of these rats coming out. [*More frightened civilians appear, held at gunpoint.*] Did they have weapons? No? Too bad. Perhaps they couldn't get their hands on them in time. [*Pointing at one man*] You look like a communist. [*The man protests. Smashes him in the face*] Take the rest away. [*The prisoners are shoved onto the lorry, which roars off.*] Lieutenant, we've done enough. You know that. How many was it the general wanted us to get today?

OFFICER 2   I don't know, sir. About a hundred, for our unit.

OFFICER   That's right. We've got to flush this scum out quickly. Get the job over with. All in all we'll have to finish off thousands of them. Otherwise they'll come back at us. I heard the general say there would be resistance for five days, so we have to get stuck in. Short and sharp. No use treating them kindly, otherwise it'll be us at the wrong end of a bullet. They had Plan Z lined up for us.

OFFICER 2 Yes, sir. What now, sir?

OFFICER You go back to barracks. We must have dealt with nearly a hundred of these fuckers today. There's going to be an official announcement this evening.

[*The officer gets into a jeep and is driven off. Soldiers follow him in a lorry.*]

Scene 2 *A television studio in Santiago. The new military Junta, seated around a table. General Pinochet, commander of the Army, flanked by Admiral Merino (Navy) and General Leigh (Air Force). All are wearing dark glasses. Martial music.*

ANNOUNCER The new authorities in Chile have an important announcement to make. Please listen attentively.

PINOCHET People of Chile! The Armed Forces of Chile, after a unanimous decision, have taken power after three years of putting up with the Marxist cancer which was destroying the moral and social order of this country and which we could no longer tolerate. The Armed Forces, representing law and order, went into action today, inspired by the patriotic impulse to rescue the country from the grave crisis into which the Marxist government of Salvador Allende was plunging it. I am speaking first as the head of Chile's biggest and oldest armed service. I have no pretentions to lead the military Junta. Now it is me, tomorrow it will be Admiral Merino, then General Leigh.

Salvador Allende is dead. He was offered an Air Force plane to fly him out of Chile. He refused to leave and committed suicide. We are the government of Chile now. There is no point in opposing the Chilean Armed Forces. Five Marxist prisoners will be shot for every soldier killed. Anyone bearing arms will be arrested and, if they resist, shot. A curfew has been decreed until it becomes unnecessary. Anyone disregarding this curfew is liable to arrest and, if they resist, execution. [*Martial music*]

Scene 3 *A few months after the coup. The house of working class people in Santiago. Knocking on the door.*

DANIEL [*going to the door*] Who is it?

VOICE It's me, Jorge, with Miguel. [*Daniel opens the door slowly and lets two men in.*]

DANIEL Great to see you. Are you alright? [*Indicating a woman behind him*] This is Juana. She's in my party. [*The two men embrace Juana.*] Sit down. Let's have some coffee. [*Juana disappears into the kitchen.*] Did you make sure you weren't followed?

MIGUEL   Quite sure. We've had plenty of experience.

DANIEL   What about that baker woman on the corner? She works for the DINA, you know.

MIGUEL   We passed by her shop, but there was only a young boy behind the counter.

JORGE   They say the DINA has thousands of people working full time for it, and three times that number of informers.

DANIEL   [*bitterly*] Some of them working class.

MIGUEL   Not many, but quite a few *lumpen*.

DANIEL   Like that cow on the corner. Before she got her shop, she was one of the local whores. [*A knock on the door. Daniel looks closely through a slit in the door.*] It's José, one of my neighbours. He's okay. [*Opens the door to a chubby little man*] Come in, José. These are friends of mine. [*José shakes hands with them all.*] Sit down. José was a Christian Democrat.

JOSÉ   *Was* is right. No more. When the coup happened and they started killing and torturing people, and Frei and Aylwin congratulated the Junta, I left. You remember what they called them? 'Military saviours of the fatherland. Heroes in uniform'. How low can you sink?

JORGE They thought the *milicos* would hand over power to them. After all, they had done everything to bring Allende down in Congress and had just been waiting for the Armed Forces to get rid of him. But not all of the Christian Democrat leaders are like that. Tomic supported Allende in many things. And Leighton asked for a *habeas corpus* for the People's Unity leaders a day after the coup. He had to leave the country after that.

JOSÉ This country has never seen such savagery. And Pinochet calls himself a Catholic. I'm a Catholic, you know.

MIGUEL Still?

JOSÉ Yes, I believe in God.

DANIEL When he allows Pinochet to do what he's done? Thousands of people killed. Many more tortured. If I was a believer, I'd say the Junta was inspired by the devil, in league with the Americans. All that talk about Allende's 'Plan Z', an internal coup, which the military had to pre-empt, it's all lies. Pinochet himself admitted there was hardly any evidence for 'Plan Z'.

JOSÉ Pinochet and his crowd'll get what they deserve eventually. Don't worry. This kind of butchery always gets punished in the end. I hate to say this, but it was partly the fault of Allende and People's Unity. Allende was a very good man, decent and upright and he stuck it out right till the end. Nobody, not even Pinochet, believes that story about his suicide. But he was playing with fire all the time. He thought he could pull everything off through sheer sleight of hand. He didn't realize what he was up against. Or if he did, he should have backed down before the coup, and thousands of people would have been saved. I think he wanted to cut a figure. You know, go down in history as a people's hero.

MIGUEL I heard that just before the coup he was going to call a referendum on the Social Area problem, as a last way out of the deadlock with Congress. He never wanted civil war, and in that my party backed him up to the hilt.

DANIEL Yes, he seemed more like a Chilean communist than some of the hotheads in his own party. I always opposed the hothead line, as you know. All that shouting for the armed struggle. Well, they certainly got their opportunity, and when it came, where were they? Totally unprepared. No arms, no training, no organization of any kind. Just rhetoric, posturing. The workers were left helpless. They were always saying: 'We are millions, and they are only a few', but the other side had the weapons, the organization and the training, and they soon broke our resistance.

MIGUEL And they are fascists, savage animals. No

morals, no scruples. Remember that Pinochet swore to execute five Marxists for every soldier killed. All that language of 'the Marxist cancer'. Not to mention the tortures.

JORGE I heard that a lot of the torturers had been trained by foreigners. Brazilians, Paraguayans, and so on.

JOSÉ Are you saying that Chileans have to be taught how to torture? In the early days after the coup they did it well enough.

DANIEL That's true. Do you remember Ana Montilla, Miguel? That girl in the MIR living in this neighbourhood. Miguel and I used to argue with her, José. Well, she was taken to the National Stadium. Her sister was picked up at the same time and released after a while, she told me. Now nobody knows where Ana is. Disappeared.

JORGE You mean they've 'disappeared' her.

DANIEL Right, poor kid. Well, in the National Stadium she was stripped and interrogated naked, like other women there. They gave her electric shocks to her mouth, hands, nipples, and vagina. They threw water over her all the time to make the pain worse. They made her repeat: 'I am a cunt. I am a cunt. I am a Marxist whore. I am a Marxist whore.' It was done on the cycle track, where they'd put up a torture chamber. One bastard even ejaculated into her mouth. They said: 'You're going to suck cock for General Pinochet, you shitty whore.' They stuck their fingers in her vagina. You can't imagine.

MIGUEL   Víctor Jara was finished off in the Chile stadium. They broke his hands and then machine-gunned him. His widow's still here, in Chile. An English woman, a dancer.

JORGE   When the Navy got a prisoner, they broke his legs and crushed his testicles. Some prisoners were held on a ship in Valparaíso harbour, killed and thrown into the sea. The Army put cigarettes out on people's bodies and gave them electric shocks on their ears, arms, and testicles. When they wanted to get rid of people altogether, they took them up in a helicopter and dropped them into the Pacific. Or shot them and buried them in mass graves.

MIGUEL   They're probably still doing it now, only there aren't as many prisoners. But bodies are still turning up in the Mapocho River. The Pinochet regime stinks in the eyes of people abroad, and they've had to let up a bit. There've even been protests in the United States. I heard that a couple of young Americans were tortured and 'executed'.

JOSÉ   The whole thing's been a disaster for Chile. But

why did Allende think he could make so many businessmen lose so much money? You know, by fixing wages and prices, and by taking over businesses that weren't playing the game and being deliberately run down by their owners. I know that, constitutionally speaking, he was within the law, but he should have known that the backlash would be terrible. Pinochet was a nobody in Prats' time, and look what a monster he became. Nobody knew he was in on the coup till it actually happened. Merino, Leigh, and Arellano Stark were probably the ones who set the whole thing up.

JORGE Do you remember what Pinochet said on the evening of the coup? That he had no ambitions to be leader of the Junta. That they would rotate power. Two days later he proclaimed himself head of the Junta and now he seems on the way to becoming President of the Republic. He closed Congress, banned all Marxist parties, and indefinitely suspended all the others.

MIGUEL Evil bastard. But I agree with José. Pinochet is a monster, but the whole situation created him. The economic problems when the Americans tried to stop other countries from buying our copper. The fall in copper prices, probably engineered by the Americans as well. We in the Communist Party tried to forge an informal alliance with the Christian Democrats, as you know, at least with their left-wing elements, the progressive, decent people. But there were so many people on the far left calling for the armed struggle, more or less defying the Armed Forces to stage a coup. And it was all rhetoric, because what did those people have to fight with? They had very few arms and even less organization. The whole idea was that the people would in the end stand up to the *golpistas*. But how?

DANIEL You know how, the General Strike. Occupation of the work places. And what occupations there were got flushed out in a couple of days by the *milicos*. There was a little bit of armed resistance in the Technical University and a few factories, and that was that.

MIGUEL *'El pueblo unido, jamás será vencido.'* Possibly true, but what we had was not People's Unity, but People's Disunity. Even Allende was getting disillusioned by the lack of support he was getting from the parties in our coalition. Every party with its own agenda and its own ways of organizing. Every party grabbing what it could for itself and jealous of the others. And when the plotters forced Prats out, it was the end.

DANIEL In the long run, those bastards were more intelligent than us. Prats was practically the only decent high-up in the military. He was solid to the end for the Constitution, non-intervention by the *milicos*, but the military behind him were not, with a couple of exceptions.

JORGE Yes, Pickering and Sepúlveda, who resigned when Prats did. They saw what was coming. Mendoza went over to the Junta and took the *Carabineros* away from Allende. They were Allende's last hope.

DANIEL But there must have been some soldiers, and even officers, who opposed the coup.

MIGUEL They got purged beforehand. Shot. I don't know how many. The most important officer on our side was that Air Force general, what's his name, Bachelet. I heard he was tortured and that he may be dead.

JOSÉ Tell me what happened to Pablo Neruda.

MIGUEL He came back from Paris with prostate cancer. After the coup they kept him for four days in Isla Negra with no medicine and wrecked his house there. Then they let him go to hospital in Santiago, where he died. They also wrecked his house in Santiago. His widow had his body taken from hospital in Santiago to his house there so that people should know what had happened to him. I went to his funeral. There weren't many of us at all. I myself was scared. But for some reason, they never came for me afterwards. You remember what Pinochet said about Neruda at the time: 'Pablo Neruda is not dead and is free. We do not kill anybody. If Neruda dies, it will be a natural death.' A natural death.

JORGE Tell me something, Miguel. As a Communist Party member, you must know why Neruda had so much trouble with the Cubans. He was practically *persona non grata* there before the coup. Why was that?

MIGUEL I'll tell you. All you leftist hotheads in the Socialist Party, the MAPU and the MIR were preaching the policy of the armed struggle after the Cuban model, when it was completely inappropriate for our country, as we can see now. Neruda was a faithful Communist Party militant and so was against that line. He became a communist in the forties, when Fidel Castro was still an adolescent, so he wasn't going to let Fidel Castro tell him what to do. He was old left, and Fidel Castro was new left, who thought he knew it all, that the only thing you had to do was go off into the mountains with a few pop-guns and make a revolution to change society. But Batista was not the Chilean upper class, and Chile was never Cuba, whatever it's become now.

JOSÉ Was it a good idea of Allende to invite Fidel Castro when he did, at the end of 1971? You remember that that was when the right first raised its head after Allende took power. The pots and pans demonstration by all those women in fur coats in the *Barrio Alto*.

MIGUEL Allende had to invite him because Fidel Castro was an ally. He put it off for a year, as you know, but in the end Fidel Castro came. But the right must have certainly seen it as a provocation. I heard that what he saw here had him worried. He thought that the country was out of control.

JORGE I wonder what advice he gave Allende.

MIGUEL It's difficult to know. There wasn't a lot he could do to help old Chicho. Even the Soviet Union more or less refused him aid. The Russians had problems of their own, and in any case were trying to arrange a *détente* with the USA.

JOSÉ Well, maybe international opinion will get rid of Pinochet. But the Americans are certainly backing him. After all, he did their job for them. They're pouring money into the country. To the government, of course. None of it's going to benefit the ordinary person.

DANIEL I think we're all lucky to be alive. And I don't see what we can do. So many people are out of work. No political parties allowed. All left-wing books banned and burned. The only people that are okay are the ones in power, and they don't know what they're doing. All they know is how to repress. You don't think that Pinochet and all the rest of those bastards have any brains, do you? Even Frei and Aylwin are grumbling now. They don't count any more. [*Juana comes in with a tray of coffee and some bread and biscuits. The men eat hungrily.*]

Scene 4 *General Carlos Prats' assassination (1)*

A street in Palermo, Buenos Aires. A night at the end of September 1974, a year after the coup. An apartment block. Two people, an American man (Michael Townley) and his wife, a Chilean woman (Mariana Inés Calleja), both DINA agents, are watching the block from a parked Renault. A car arrives, a grey Fiat 125, driven by exiled Chilean General Carlos Prats. It enters the garage. Another car enters and Townley slips into the garage with a canvas bag. Prats and the other car-owner go upstairs to their flats. Silence. Townley is left alone in the garage. Steps of someone coming into the garage from the inside are heard. It is a caretaker. Townley lies low on the floor and then slips behind a boiler. The caretaker looks around then goes away. Townley waits, then takes a pistol and his documents from the bag and puts them on a ledge. He then takes a package from the bag. It is a bomb. Townley slips under the grey Fiat to place the bomb under the transmission. He emerges, picks up the bag, his documents and pistol, puts them in the bag and goes to the garage door, which is locked. He tries to open it in vain, and curses. He goes back behind the boiler to wait.

Scene 5 *General Carlos Prats' assassination (2)*

Late evening the next day. Prats and his wife Sofía are dining with their friends Ramón and Panchita Huidobro, in the Huidobros' apartment.

RAMÓN HUIDOBRO Well, General, the film was good, wasn't it?

SOFÍA PRATS And Carlos didn't want to go at first. 'Water and Chocolate' didn't appeal to him as a title.

CARLOS PRATS It was fine. Ugo Tognazzi was splendid.

RAMÓN HUIDOBRO General, this is all very well, but the situation for you here is dangerous. I heard from my friends in the Argentinian military that you are being watched by the military attached to the Chilean embassy. Pinochet thinks you're a threat to him.

CARLOS PRATS That skunk. And it was myself who recommended him to President Allende. Who would have believed that he would be one of the leaders of the coup? Our families were friendly. Allende trusted him. But he's not having things all his own way. I heard that Leigh has protested at Pinochet's idea of making himself President. Leigh and Merino were the public threat. Pinochet was a wolf in sheep's clothing. And now he's top dog.

SOFÍA PRATS Carlos has just finished his memoirs and we are thinking of leaving for Madrid. We're waiting for a Chilean passport.

PANCHITA HUIDOBRO Do you really think they'll

give you one?

RAMÓN HUIDOBRO The Argentinians will give you a passport.

CARLOS PRATS I'm a Chilean general, and I can't travel on a foreign passport.

PANCHITA HUIDOBRO You really should accept their offer. Ramón is really worried about you.

CARLOS PRATS There may be something in what you say. A Chilean military officer here warned me that Pinochet was going to have me assassinated by Croats. It didn't seem likely to me. But I'll think about it. You may be right.

Scene 6 *General Carlos Prats' assassination (3)*

Just after midnight the same night, outside the block of flats in the Palermo area where the Prats couple live. The Prats' drive up in their grey Fiat 125 and Carlos Prats gets out to open the garage door. The Renault with Townley and his wife can be seen parked across the street. Prats gets back into his car and Mariana Inés Townley tries to activate to remote control apparatus to set off the bomb. She fails.

TOWNLEY What the fuck are you doing? Doesn't the thing work? [*Takes it from her*] You idiot, the safety catch is on. [*He moves the safety catch and presses a button. A vast explosion. Sofía Prats is thrown from the front right-hand seat of the Prats' car. Her husband is thrown out on the left. After the smoke clears, only pieces of their bodies can be seen, scattered around the area.*]

Scene 7 *Santiago. One of the torture centers set up by the military Junta. A man is brought in, between two soldiers, who take him to an army officer seated behind a desk.*

OFFICER [*Looking through some papers. Politely*] We have a lot of information on you. Your wife and your daughter have been arrested. We need some information on members of your party. Alfonso Guzmán and Jaime Tomás. I believe they are quite high up and that you know them well. They were always talking about infiltrating the Armed Forces.

PRISONER I know them by sight, but I wasn't a friend.

OFFICER But you were a comrade. [*Smiles*] We need addresses for them, where they're hiding.

PRISONER I don't know.

OFFICER I told you we have arrested your wife and daughter. If you don't believe me, we can bring them here. You have to understand, I have all powers from General Pinochet to do whatever I want with you and your family.

PRISONER I don't know where those two men are.

OFFICER Okay. [*Beckons to two soldiers, who punch and kick the prisoner until he screams.*] Now what? Where are they?

PRISONER I don't know.

OFFICER You don't know? [*Shouting*] You Marxist son of a whore, you'll tell me even if I have to kill you. [*To the soldiers*] Give him the treatment. [*They haul the prisoner to the side of the room, where there is a bed with a metal frame and no mattress. They blindfold him and strip him naked, handcuff him, and strap him onto the bed. The straps are connected to a small electricity generator. A bucket of water is thrown over him. The generator is switched on. The man convulses and screams, howling frantically. After twenty seconds, one of the torturers flips the current off. The prisoner is sobbing like a child.*] Well, where are they? Come on, you bastard, you know.

PRISONER [*trembling*] I may be able to take you to

them. But please don't hurt my wife and daughter.

OFFICER That all depends on you, my friend. [*To the torturers*] Get him up and clothed, and tell the two soldiers that brought him to escort him to where his friends are. Then you pick them up and bring them here. [*The prisoner is taken away. Another is ushered in, between soldiers. The man is sobbing and pleading.*]

CURTAIN

ACT 2

Scene 1 *President Pinochet's office in Santiago de Chile. June 8, 1976. Noon. A meeting during the Organization of American States' conference. Pinochet, Patricio Carvajal, Pinochet's Foreign Minister, Manuel Trucco, his Ambassador to the United States, Ricardo Claro, the Chilean OAS conference coordinator, Henry Kissinger, U.S. Secretary of State, William D. Rogers, Assistant Secretary for Inter-American Affairs. Kissinger and Pinochet speak through an interpreter.*

KISSINGER This is a beautiful building. The conference is well organized. Are you meeting with all the delegations?

PINOCHET Yes, two or three a day. I want to tell you we are grateful that you have come to the conference.

KISSINGER It is an honour. I was touched by the popular reception when I arrived. I have a strong feeling of friendship in Chile.

PINOCHET This is a country of warm-hearted people, who love liberty. This is the reason they did not accept communism when the communists attempted to take over the country. It is a long-term struggle we are part of. It is a further stage of the same conflict which erupted into the Spanish Civil War. And we note the fact that though the Spaniards tried to stop communism 40 years ago, it is springing up again in Spain.

KISSINGER We had the Spanish King recently, and I discussed that very issue with him.

PINOCHET I have always been against communism. During the Vietnam War, I met with some of your military and made my anti-communism clear to them, and told them I hoped they could bring about its defeat.

KISSINGER In Vietnam, we defeated ourselves through our internal divisions. There is a worldwide propaganda campaign by the communists.

PINOCHET Chile is suffering from that propaganda effort. Unfortunately, we do not have the millions of dollars needed for counter-propaganda.

KISSINGER In the United States, as you know, we are sympathetic to what you are trying to do here. I think that the previous government was headed toward communism. We wish your government well. At the same time, we face massive domestic problems, in all branches of the government, especially Congress, but also in the Executive, over the issue of human rights. Even my own State Department is made up of people who have a vocation for the ministry. Because there are not enough churches for them, they went into the Department of State. As you know, Congress is debating further restraints on aid to Chile. We are opposed. But basically we don't want to intervene in your domestic affairs. We can't be precise in our proposals about what you should do. But this is a problem that complicates our relationships and the efforts of those who are friends of Chile. I am going to speak about human rights this afternoon in the General Assembly. I delayed my statement until I could talk to you. I wanted you to understand my position. We want to deal in moral persuasion, not by legal sanctions. It is for this reason that we oppose the Kennedy Amendment. In my statement, I will treat human rights in general terms, and human rights in a world context. I will refer in two paragraphs to the report on Chile of the OAS Human Rights Commission. I will say that the human rights issue has impaired relations between the U.S. and Chile. This is partly the result of congressional actions. I will add that I hope you will shortly remove those obstacles. The speech is not aimed at Chile. I wanted to tell you about this. My evaluation is that you are a victim of all left-wing groups around the world, and that your greatest sin was that you overthrew a government that was going communist.

PINOCHET I understand.

KISSINGER It would really help if you would let us

know the measures you are taking in the human rights field. None of this is said in the hope of undermining your government. I want you to succeed, and I want to retain the possibility of aid. If we defeat the Kennedy Amendment—I don't know if you listen in on my phone, but if you do, you have just heard me issue instructions to Washington to make an all-out effort to do just that. If we defeat it, we will deliver the F-5E's as we agreed to.

PINOCHET   We are returning to institutionalization step by step. But we are constantly being attacked by the Christian Democrats. They have a strong voice in Washington. Not the people in the Pentagon, but they do get through to Congress. Gabriel Valdés has access. Also Letelier.

KISSINGER   I have not seen a Christian Democrat for years.

PINOCHET   Also Tomic, and others I don't recall. Letelier has access to Congress. We know they are giving false information. You see, we have no experience in government. We are worried about our image. In a few days, we will publish the constitutional article on human rights, and also another setting up the Council of State. In the economic area, we have paid our debts, after the renegotiation. We are paying $700 million in debts with interest this year. We have made land reforms. We have freed most detained prisoners. On September 11, 1974 I

114

challenged the Soviets to set free their prisoners. But they haven't done so, while we have only 400 people who are now detained. In international relations we are doing well. In the case of Bolivia, we have extended our good will. It all depends now on Peru.

KISSINGER I have the impression that Peru is not very sympathetic.

PINOCHET Peru is arming. Peru is trying to buy a carrier from the British for $160 million. It is also building four torpedo boats in Europe. Peru is breaking the arms balance in the South Pacific. It has 600 tanks from the Soviet Union. We are doing what we can to sustain ourselves in case of an emergency.

KISSINGER What are you doing?

PINOCHET We are largely modifying old armaments, fixing junked units. We are a people with energy. We have no Indians.

KISSINGER I gather Chile generally wins its wars.

PINOCHET We have never lost a war. We are a proud people. On the human rights front, we are slowly making progress. We are now down to 400. We have freed more. And we are also changing some sentences so that the prisoners may be eligible to leave.

KISSINGER You could group the releases: instead of 20 a week, have a bigger program of releases. That would be better for their psychological power. My statement and our position are designed to allow us to say to Congress that we are talking to the Chilean government and, therefore, Congress need not act. We thought it better for Chile if I came. My statement is not offensive to Chile. Ninety-five per cent of what I say is applicable to all the governments in the hemisphere. We want an outcome that is not deeply embarrassing to you. But as friends, I must tell you that we face a situation in the United States where we must be able to point to events here in Chile, or we will be defeated.

PINOCHET How does the U.S. see the problem between Chile and Peru?

KISSINGER [*after a pause*] We would not like to see a conflict. Much depends on who begins it. The American people would ask who is advancing on whom.

PINOCHET But you know what's going on here. You see it with your satellites.

KISSINGER Well, I can assure you that if you take Lima, you will have little U.S. support.

PINOCHET We did it once, a hundred years ago. It would be difficult now, in view of the present balance of forces.

KISSINGER If Peru attacked, this would be a serious matter for a country armed with Soviet equipment. It would be serious. Clearly we would oppose it diplomatically. But it all depends, beyond that. It is not easy to generate support for U.S. military action these days.

PINOCHET We must fight with our own arms?

KISSINGER It depends how it happens.

PINOCHET Assume the worst, that is to say, that Chile is the aggressor. Peru defends itself, and then attacks us. What happens?

KISSINGER It's not that easy. We will know who the aggressor is. If you are not the aggressor, then you will have support.

CARVAJAL In the case of Bolivia, if we give Bolivia some territory, Bolivian territory might be guaranteed by the American states.

KISSINGER I have supported Bolivia in its aspirations to the sea, but De la Flor is not happy about it.

CARVAJAL If we gave some territory to Bolivia, and then permitted Peru to use the port, Peru would get everything it needs.

KISSINGER It is my feeling Peru will not accept.

PINOCHET I am concerned very much by the Peruvian situation. Circumstances might produce aggression by Peru. Why are they buying tanks? They have heavy artillery, 155s. Peru is more inclined to Russia than to the U.S. Russia supports their people one hundred per cent. We are behind you. You are the leader, but you have a punitive system for your friends.

KISSINGER There is merit in what you say. It is a curious time in the U.S. It is unfortunate. We have been through Vietnam and Watergate. We have to wait until after the elections. We welcomed the overthrow of the communist-inclined government here. We are not out to weaken your position. On foreign aggression, it would be a grave situation if one were attacked. That would constitute a direct threat to the inter-American system.

CARVAJAL There is massive Cuban influence in Peru. Many Cubans are there. The Peruvians may be pushed. And what happens to the thousands of Cuban soldiers now in Africa, when they are no longer needed there?

KISSINGER If there are Cuban troops involved in a Peruvian attack, then the problem is easy. We will not permit a Cuban military force of 5,000 Cubans in Peru.

CARVAJAL There is the danger of irresponsible attack.

There is a real chance that Cuba could airlift troops to Peru.

KISSINGER The Cubans are not good soldiers. And if there were an airlift, the question is then easy. We will not permit Cuba another military adventure. A war between Peru and Chile would be a complex thing, but in a war between Cuba and Chile or others, we would not be indifferent. After the election, we will have massive trouble if they are not out of Angola. We can't accept coexistence and ideological subversion. We have the conditions now for a more realistic policy. It would help you if you had some human rights progress, which could be announced in packages. Give us advance information about these measures. As for the Christian Democrats, we are not using them. I haven't seen one since 1969. I want to see our relations and friendship improve. I encouraged the OAS to have its General Assembly here. I knew it would add prestige to Chile. I came for that reason. We have suggestions. We want to help, not undermine you. You did a great service to the West in overthrowing Allende. Otherwise, Chile would have followed Cuba. Then there would have been no human rights or a Human Rights Commission. And now we have to help the Argentinian military. I'd like to see their terrorism problem solved by the end of the year.

Scene 2 *Michael Townley's house in Lo Curro, Santiago. The phone rings. Townley picks it up.*

TOWNLEY You've picked up Carmelo Soria and are bringing him here? Okay. [*To a chauffeur*] Héctor, tell the plumber to stop work and leave. [*To his secretary*] You leave too, please, Alejandra. A special unit will be here shortly. [*She leaves. Plain-clothes police bring in a prisoner. The latter is blindfolded and his hands are tied.*]

DINA AGENT 1 Who do you know in the Chilean Communist Party? Who are your contacts there? [*Beating him*]

DINA AGENT 2 Where does the party get its money from? [*Punching the prisoner in the face*] What about its weapons?

CARMELO SORIA Poor Chile.

DINA AGENT 1 Talk, you piece of Marxist shit, or we'll make you wish you'd never been born. [*Slapping him*]

DINA AGENT 2 We've been watching you. The money has been coming in a diplomatic bag, hasn't it? Come on, you cunt, answer me.

CARMELO SORIA Poor Chile.

DINA AGENT 1   Don't try and hide anything. Don't lie to us, you swine. We've been following you for a long time. Your wife's having an affair with another man. Didn't you know?

CAPTAIN   [*to Agent 1*] Go upstairs to the office and type up the letter. Type an envelope with his name on it. Carmelo Soria. [*Agent 1 leaves. The captain lights a cigarette. The prisoner is silent. After a while, Agent 1 comes downstairs with the letter.*] I want you two men to prepare an accident for this man. You are to go to *La Pirámide* near the canal. You know where that is? You stand guard there. Make sure nobody enters the area. Understand? Okay, off you go. [*The two torturers leave. To other agents*] Strap him to the bed. [*To the prisoner*] Drink. [*Forcing him to drink from a bottle of pisco. After the first swallows, the prisoner gasps.*] No, more, you son of a bitch, drink the whole fucking lot. [*Ramming the bottle in the prisoner's mouth again*] Okay, give him the treatment. [*All the other agents join in beating and punching him savagely. The prisoner bleeds profusely.*]

TOWNLEY   [*entering the room*] Can't you make less noise? The neighbours can hear all this. [*They beat him a bit more, then stop. The captain unstraps him from the bed, and with the help of two of his men, drags Carmelo to a stone staircase of four steps. He props Carmelo's head against the edge of one of the steps and gives him a karate chop in the neck. Carmelo's spine cracks and he*

121

dies. In the meantime, he has kept totally silent.]

CAPTAIN   Okay, he's dead. Damned foreigner. You know he was a *coño*, a shitty Spaniard, with Chilean nationality. An international subversive. Put him back on the bed. Take his watch, but leave him his wallet with some money in it. Take him out to the VW and splash *pisco* around inside. Then take him off to *La Pirámide* and drive the car into the canal. Leave the *pisco* bottle outside the car. Leave his jacket near his body with the letter in it. It's proof of his wife's infidelity. When you've finished, come back here and we'll ring *Mamo* Contreras to tell him the operation has been carried out.

Scene 3   *A worker's house in Santiago. On the wall is a crucifix and an image of the Virgin Mary.*

JOSÉ   I can't offer you very much, my friends. Just tea and sandwiches.

JORGE   I feel like a drop of wine.

JOSÉ   Oh, there's plenty of that, but go easy on it, Jorge. People have been telling me you're drinking too much.

JORGE   What can you do? No job, no money, and these military bastards still in power.

JOSÉ There's too many working-class Chileans boozing themselves to death.

JORGE There always have been. Wine's still cheap here.

JOSÉ Don't you realize that's what the *milicos* want? [*Calls into the kitchen*] María, have we got anything else to drink?

MARÍA [*emerging from the kitchen*] Just a bit of lemonade. There might be a drop of coffee left. Who's it for?

JOSÉ Jorge.

MARÍA [*to Jorge*] Oh, what'll you have, dear?

JORGE Coffee.

JOSÉ That's the stuff, man. [*A knock. He goes to the door, looks through the spy-hole, undoes the chain, and lets some people in. They are Daniel, Juana, and Miguel.*] Welcome, lads. And you too, Juana. How's it going in the shop?

JUANA Just making ends meet.

JOSÉ Sit down. Make yourselves comfortable. [*María*

passes round the refreshments.] Miguel, you're still free.

MIGUEL Just about. They could come at any moment. You know they arrested Daniel?

DANIEL Nothing really, just for a couple of days. They didn't torture me or even beat me up.

JOSÉ What did they want?

DANIEL You'll have to laugh. Information about Altamirano. As if I had ever had anything to do with him.

MIGUEL Good thing too, that idiot. They must be going after him.

DANIEL He's most likely abroad. Too dangerous for him here.

JORGE They'll get him with a bomb. Like they did Prats and Letelier. Pinochet's a real monster. He even had the gall to have Letelier killed in Washington. That can't have gone down well with the Yanks. There's bound to be a reaction. You see how stupid Pinochet is. Perhaps they'll try and gun Altamirano down on the street, as they did to Leighton in Italy. Leighton was one of the best men in your party, José.

JOSÉ My former party, you mean. Thank God he's still

alive. Although a lot of the worst ones have finally woken up to what this lot are all about.

DANIEL A little late, wouldn't you say?

JORGE They're even complaining about the 'Chicago Boys'. Even those right-wing Christian Democrats, the ones that went on an international tour just after the coup to whip up support for the Junta, don't like what's happening now. 'Economic freedom must precede political freedom.' Let the rich take over completely and then we'll see about political freedom, when we're all begging for slaves' jobs. Everything done by decree now, ever since they abolished political parties. Most of the nationalized industries sold off.

JOSÉ Not the copper industry, though. Pinochet didn't dare. But he gave the Americans handsome compensation for what Allende's government did.

JUANA Allende sent them packing with the full support of Congress.

DANIEL Yes, those were the days. It's all been turned on its head now. Practically no public spending, mass unemployment, and let the last man starve. I read that Chile is a kind of guinea pig for Friedman's policies. Nowhere else would dare apply them, not even the USA. You know how much Friedman got for his little lecture tour here last year? Thirty thousand U.S. dollars, for just six day's work.

JORGE But he certainly convinced Pinochet. Not that Pinochet knows anything about economics.

DANIEL Or anything else, except how to torture and kill. Caravans of Death and Operation Condors are his stuff.

JUANA And how to betray his democratically elected president. Poor old Chicho. He didn't know what hit him. And now it's happening in Argentina. God help them there if it's the same kind of people as these bastards here.

MIGUEL We'll just have to stick it out. Not let ourselves get killed. Try to maintain our party structures. Now that Nixon's gone, perhaps the Yanks will let up a bit.

DANIEL I can't see it. Whatever president they have, their foreign policy interests are the same. It's just a choice between hard-pedal and soft-pedal.

MARÍA Okay, folks, let's let up a bit on the politics. We're here to celebrate José's birthday. Get stuck in.

JORGE I propose a toast to the most radical and decent

Christian Democrat in Chile.

JOSÉ Ex-Christian Democrat.

JORGE But you still have the crucifix on your wall. You're still a Catholic.

JOSÉ Yes, I am.

DANIEL Well, get on the hotline to God and ask him when he's going to deal out justice to these torturers and murderers.

JUANA Don't be so rude, Daniel. It's José's birthday.

JOSÉ Don't worry, dear, I can see what he means. But it won't last forever, you'll all see.

MIGUEL I should hope not. Cheers for José, anyway.

ALL [*raising their cups and glasses*] Cheers.

INTERLUDE I

In November 1976, the Democrat Jimmy Carter wins the elections in the USA, after the Watergate scandal that led to President Nixon's resignation and the Ford government, which still included Kissinger. One of the main planks in Carter's campaign was the human rights issue, and the Pinochet government has to be more careful about what it is doing to wipe out its opponents. The car-bomb killing of Allende's former Minister Orlando Letelier and his assistant Ronni Moffitt, a young American woman, in Washington just before Jimmy Carter's electoral victory, has created an enormous scandal in the United States and caused much previously unconcerned American public opinion to regard the Pinochet regime with horror.

In 1978, Pinochet passes an amnesty law, in an attempt to bury the crimes committed by his regime. He starts to distance himself from his most notorious henchman, Lt. Colonel Manuel Contreras, the head of DINA, which is dissolved, replaced by the CNI (National Information Centre). General Leigh is dismissed from the Junta. A new constitution is promulgated in Chile in 1980, approved by a dubiously conducted referendum, allowing civilians to 'collaborate' with the military regime. This 1980 constitution provides for an Armed Forces' candidate to be President from 1989 to 1997 if he is approved by a further referendum to be held in late 1988. If the vote goes against this candidate, a civilian may become President, thus paving the way for a democracy. It is taken as read that the Junta of Armed Forces commanders-in-chief are going to select Pinochet as their candidate.

In February 1982, Tucapel Jiménez, a trade union leader, is found assassinated in a car. He had been shot in the head and garroted, with his head practically severed from his body. In March 1985, three Chilean university lecturers are found decapitated. In 1986, an attempt is made on Pinochet's life by the Manuel Rodríguez Patriotic Front, behind which is the Chilean Communist Party, at last roused from its slumbers to take drastic measures against the tyrant. The attack, made with anti-tank missiles on a Pinochet motorcade, fails to kill the target, but leaves five dead and twelve wounded. Six militants of the Chilean Communist Party are arrested and executed.

Scene 4 *La Moneda. 1 a.m. on the night of 5-6 October 1988. The results of the referendum of October 5 have been declared to decide whether Pinochet stays in power as President, or if a civilian government will be voted in after one year. Pinochet has lost the referendum. Four members of the Junta: General Fernando Matthei (Air Force); General Rodolfo Stange (Carabineros); General Humberto Gordon (CNI-State Security); and Admiral José Toribio Merino (Navy) meet with President Pinochet, Minister of the Interior Sergio Fernández, and Cabinet Secretary Sergio Valenzuela.*

PINOCHET Gentlemen, I have called this meeting because we have a problem, which you no doubt know about. Minister Fernández, could you explain?

FERNÁNDEZ Yes, Mr. President. It appears that the opposition vote in yesterday's referendum was slightly larger than the vote for President Pinochet. The official figures are 43% as against 54.7%. This is hardly decisive and the President thinks that in view of the instability that will be created if he steps down, this vote can be overruled.

MATTHEI Overruled? But that is to go against the 1980 Constitution that President Pinochet himself established. I was asked by the press just before coming into this meeting what was going to happen, and I told the reporters that it looked as if the NO vote had won and that the whole Junta would discuss this with President Pinochet. I must admit that this vote has surprised me, but we have to respect it.

PINOCHET We cannot allow this country to slide back into its old ways, with politicians in power. I am asking you for special emergency powers. I want troops out on the street to take over Santiago until we sort this matter out. I have prepared a document to this effect requiring the signatures of all the members of the Junta.

MATTHEI General Pinochet, we cannot agree to these

extraordinary measures. You cannot just overturn your own constitution. You as the Armed Forces' candidate have lost and you must do what the Constitution says. Hand over power to a civilian president after elections in one year's time.

PINOCHET Have you any idea of what this will mean? I saved the country in 1973 and now we're going to have to hand it over to some of those politicians that were dragging it to ruin. I must have special powers.

MATTHEI General, everybody knows what you did to stop the communists. We all backed you. But times have changed. Even without you as president, the country will continue on the track you laid down.

PINOCHET I can hardly believe you're saying this, Matthei. Remember it was me that appointed you to the Junta after I had to kick Leigh out. How can you be so disloyal?

MATTHEI It is not disloyalty, General. You have to play by your own rules.

PINOCHET [*nearly apoplectic*] Rules, rules. You're talking like Allende. Look where the rules got *him*. Admiral Merino, what do you say?

MERINO I have to support General Matthei. You

cannot go against your own rules. We have lost the referendum, but we have lost honorably. If we do what you want, we shall still have lost, but also cover ourselves in shame. And the document you are showing us purports to be the minutes of this meeting, when the meeting is still not over.

STANGE   General, I too have to support General Matthei and Admiral Merino. We have talked about the matter already.

PINOCHET   Oh, you have, eh? And General Gordon? What about you?

GORDON   General, I agree with Generals Matthei and Stange and Admiral Merino.

PINOCHET   Oh my God. [*Valenzuela collapses.*] Look what's happened now. My own cabinet secretary having a heart attack. [*An aide takes Valenzuela away.*] Admiral Merino, I would never have expected this of you. An original member of the Junta that saved Chile.

MERINO   I'm sorry. My mind is made up, General. You cannot have your own way this time.

PINOCHET   I cannot believe what I am hearing. General Stange, we shall need more troops on the streets here to control the demonstrators.

STANGE   I think not, sir. My *Carabineros* are quite adequate.

PINOCHET   [*apoplectically*] You ungrateful swine.

CURTAIN

INTERLUDE II

In 1990, the Christian Democrat Leader Patricio Aylwin takes over the presidency in a coalition government of moderate democratic politicians, including some socialists. He immediately creates the National Commission for Truth and Reconciliation to report on the violations of human rights under the previous regime (1973-90). A year later, the report (the Rettig Report) is published. Its tentative findings show, in 2,920 cases examined, that over two thousand people were victims of human rights violations, usually meaning torture, over a thousand were dead, and just under a thousand had 'disappeared' after arrest. Aylwin is succeeded in 1994 by Eduardo Frei Ruiz-Tagle, the son of former Christian Democrat President Eduardo Frei Montalvo, Allende's predecessor. Frei junior presides over a similar government to that of Aylwin, and is in power in Chile when Pinochet is arrested in London. Under Frei, more and more charges are allowed to be brought against the military for the atrocities which had occurred under the Pinochet regime. Contreras and his subordinate Espinoza are found guilty of arranging the Letelier murder in Washington, and jailed. At the time of Pinochet's arrest in London, he has relinquished his command of the Army and is now a life senator, with immunity from prosecution in Chile.

ACT 3

Scene 1 *The United Kingdom. October 3, 1998. Pinochet is recovering in room 801 of the London Clinic from an operation for a slipped disc. There is a bedside table with a telephone, a TV, a radio, and a refrigerator.*

IRISH NURSE   Wake up, sir. [*Pinochet sits up in bed, his head resting on the backboard. The nurse, on the right-hand side of the bed, puts her hand comfortingly on Pinochet's shoulder. Four people enter, three of them police officers, and a woman interpreter.*]

DETECTIVE SERGEANT   Senator Pinochet, do you speak or understand English?

PINOCHET   [*fuzzily*] No. I can say only: my leg hurt. [*The detective sergeant shows his credentials.*]

INTERPRETER   [*to Pinochet*] *Yo soy intérprete. Este es el detective sargento Jones. Allí están el detective inspector Hewitt y el inspector jefe de la comisaría de Marylebone. ¿Me ha entendido, senador?*

PINOCHET   *Sí.*

INTERPRETER   *Por favor, escuche lo que voy a decirle.*

DETECTIVE SERGEANT Senator Pinochet, you are under arrest. You may remain silent, but if you are asked a question and do not reply to something which you want to be heard in court, it may harm your defence. Whatever you say now may be used in evidence against you.

[*Detective Inspector Hewitt prepares to take notes. The interpreter repeats the sergeant's words to Pinochet in Spanish.*]

DETECTIVE SERGEANT I have to inform you…

PINOCHET [*enraged*] *Ustedes no tienen derecho a hacer esto, no pueden arrestarme. ¡Yo estoy aquí en una misión secreta!*

INTERPRETER [*to the detective sergeant*] He says you have no right to arrest him, and that he is here on a secret mission.

DETECTIVE SERGEANT What secret mission?

PINOCHET *Yo he venido aquí en una misión secreta, tengo un pasaporte diplomático y derecho a la inmunidad. ¡No me pueden arrestar! ¡Esto es humillante! ¡Es una vergüenza que en este país me hagan esto!*

INTERPRETER [*to the detective sergeant*] He says he has a diplomatic passport and the right to immunity. He cannot be arrested. It is humiliating and a disgrace for this to be done to him in this country.

DETECTIVE SERGEANT '…there being proof that between 11 September 1973 and 31 December 1983 you did cause Spanish citizens to be murdered in Chile…'

PINOCHET *Esto es absolutamente ilegal.*

INTERPRETER *Quédese tranquilo. Me imagino que pronto va a venir aquí su embajador.*

PINOCHET *Yo sé quién está detrás de esto. Es el comunista ése de Garcés.*

DETECTIVE SERGEANT What is he saying?

INTERPRETER He's talking about a person who he thinks is behind his arrest.

PINOCHET *Esto es algo increíble, ¡no lo puedo creer!*

INTERPRETER [*trying to comfort Pinochet*] *Usted está bajo la protección de la Policía Metropolitana, senador. Buenas noches. Hasta mañana. Trate de dormir.*

PINOCHET [*resignedly*] *Buenas noches. Muchas gracias.*

Scene 2 *November 1998. Pinochet's son, Augusto Pinochet Hiriart, is interviewed in Santiago by Catalan TV from Barcelona. Augusto Pinochet Hiriart is physically very like his father. He is wearing a sober grey suit and tie.*

INTERVIEWER Mr. Pinochet, you have said that Judge Garzón is a link in a chain of socialist plots against your father. Do you believe that the British Crown Prosecution Service, the European Parliament, and other judges in European countries have been contaminated in this same way by the socialists?

PINOCHET HIRIART Yes, I would emphatically say that. For a start, one of the judges in the House of Lords who tried my father was in Chile and had a strong friendship with Allende. Because of this, he should have been disqualified, but he was allowed to sit on the tribunal.

INTERVIEWER Would you care to say something about the 'disappeared'?

PINOCHET HIRIART There are things that cannot be told. They are state secrets and there is such a thing as reason of state.

INTERVIEWER What do you have to say about secret prisons and torture?

PINOCHET HIRIART [*calmly*] There were prisons, and they were not secret. Torture centers? The methods used by the civil police before we became the government were methods established by the USA, methods of interrogation. Nowadays, these are considered as torture. Well, possibly. The methods that you used in times gone by, let us say, when you did things in the past, were also fairly cruel.

INTERVIEWER Which past are you talking about?

PINOCHET HIRIART Have you forgotten the Inquisition in Spain? [*Sarcastically, with a little grimace of satisfaction*] I have not forgotten, it's part of history. In those times, total cruelty was practiced. But nobody has put Spain on trial for that or afterwards either, for things the Spanish did when they came to America, atrocious things. But we are not protesting about that. What is past is past.

INTERVIEWER Mr. Pinochet, did you ever get nightmares after the coup of September 11, 1973 and the subsequent repression, since you must have witnessed some unpleasant acts?

PINOCHET HIRIART Nightmares before the coup, yes. After, never. It was right to shoot those people because they were fighting against us and were extremely evil people with terrible records. Enough to make your

141

hair fall out. When you read the records of those people, you realize that they were wild beasts. Not human beings.

INTERVIEWER   Ricardo Lagos has suggested that Pinochet should be sent back to Chile to face trial. Do you accept that?

PINOCHET HIRIART   I have not heard Lagos' proposals. He is such an erratic man. [*Smiles*] But in Chile, there are fourteen formal indictments against my father and that is going to be followed up. If anything can be proved against him and it is done according to proper justice, as it undoubtedly will be, if there is any sanction, if it is a rational one, my father will agree to accept it.

Scene 3   *Rio de Janeiro Summit Meeting, 27 June 1999. Juan Gabriel Valdés, Chilean Foreign Minister and Robin Cook, UK Foreign Secretary, meet in the Copacabana Palace Hotel. Both are attended by two aides.*

VALDÉS   [*smiling*] You know what we are going to talk about, don't you?

COOK   [*laughing*] I haven't the remotest idea. Tell me.

VALDÉS   The Chilean government wants to establish a frank relationship with the British government. I am not going to say anything about the arrest of your distinguished guest, but that is something very important for our political process. At the end of this year we have presidential elections. Probably, the Socialist candidate Ricardo Lagos will be the third Chilean President of the era of transition to democracy. And we want to resolve this matter as soon as possible.

COOK Very interesting. I would really like to know what is happening.

VALDÉS President Frei has spoken on the telephone to Prime Minister Tony Blair and explained to him the nature of our problem.

COOK What do you mean? Is your democracy in danger?

VALDÉS No, but the forces have polarized. We have tensions again and a wide division. Nothing dangerous. But with a new president coming to power, we are having to turn our attention once more to a past that we thought we had overcome. Also, we believe that it is Chilean justice that must judge Pinochet.

COOK I understand.

VALDÉS General Pinochet is an old man now, with health problems. We have medical reports speaking of possible complications. He is very depressed.

COOK All reports from Scotland Yard insist up to now that he is a person enjoying good health with the typical problems of an aged man. You know that he is under constant watch at home day and night.

VALDÉS Yes, I know. But I am worried about two possible catastrophic scenarios.

COOK What are they?

VALDÉS The first is that Pinochet could die in London and have to return to Santiago in a coffin. The other is Pinochet in prison in Madrid. The Armed Forces would go back to the past, and there would be an outbreak of nationalism which would harm our relations.

COOK We are not going to allow Pinochet to die in the United Kingdom.

VALDÉS Look, the Chilean government is going to monitor the general's health closely. Could we send you the medical reports?

COOK Of course. I want to tell you that in our extradition system, the decision will be taken by the Home Secretary Jack Straw, acting in a purely judicial function. He is not going to consult the Cabinet. But I can pass on to him all the information that you send us. I also want to say that we are under an obligation to Spain.

We are party to the European Extradition Agreement and they are asking for extradition.

VALDÉS You know that the Spanish government requested the extradition, but they don't want him there.

COOK If they have asked for it, how can it be that they don't want it?

VALDÉS They have sent on the judge's request, but they recognize that it would be a nightmare if you send him to Madrid.

COOK I see. I shall have to make consultations on this matter.

VALDÉS Thank you.

[*Cook and Valdés get up. Photographers enter the suite and take pictures of them sitting together on a sofa with a flower design. They shake hands.*]

Scene 4 *Rio de Janeiro, the following day. The Caesar Park Hotel on Ipanema. Eduardo Frei and José María Aznar, the Spanish Prime Minister, are meeting. Frei is accompanied by Juan Gabriel Valdés and José Miguel Insulza, Frei's new Secretary General. Aznar is attended by Abel Matutes, the Spanish Foreign Minister. Other*

*functionaries of the two governments are present. It is
more like a conference than a bilateral meeting. Aznar is
wearing a beige suit, a white shirt and matching tie. He
is a perky little tailor's dummy of a man, with a thick
moustache. He is sitting on a sofa. Frei, in a grey suit, is
seated in a French-style armchair. Between them is a
table with a tray full of fresh daisies. Some functionaries
have their notebooks out.*

INSULZA [*to Valdés*] Juan Gabriel, you don't have any
objection to my taking part in the meeting, do you, as the
previous Foreign Minister? I want to say goodbye and say
a few things.

VALDÉS Of course not.

FREI [*irritatedly, to Aznar*] Pinochet has become the
main problem in our transition after two governments,
and we have new elections in December. We always saw
Spain's transition to democracy as a model because you
tried to avoid dragging up the past. I think we needed a
real desire to settle our problem, and frankly, the Spanish
government has never shown this desire. We want to
negotiate with you politically if you want to call it by that
name, but if you reject that, it won't be possible. We want
to negotiate with you and the British. Pinochet's state of
health is complicated. He is fairly depressed and his
diabetes is getting worse. Foreign Minister Valdés has
informed me that you do not accept arbitration, and are

recommending that we put the case straight before The Hague. I don't understand how you can accept one part of the treaty and not the other. I think he should explain our position.

VALDÉS Pinochet's health is not good, and as the President has stated, we think that you are interpreting the Anti-Torture Agreement in a one-sided way. Foreign Minister Matutes is advising us to go straight to The Hague Court of International Justice, but the treaty gives a space of six months for arbitration before submitting the case to the Court. Only if an agreement is not reached does the case go to The Hague.

AZNAR [*to Frei*] Look, Eduardo, if I were in your shoes I would be just as upset as you. I have already said so publicly. I don't agree that the Spanish government should try to give lessons in democracy. And I also don't think that we have to play the role of International Court of Justice or roam the world righting wrongs. But you are wrong if you think we don't want to help matters. We want to collaborate with you. The problem is that we can't. We don't have the least leeway. And besides, we are the only ones who want to help. The socialists are not helping but continually attacking. You have contacts with the Spanish Socialist Party, and you know this because you are in coalition with the socialists in your government. Then there is the humanitarian question. I can assure you that if the British government, in the exercise of its authority, decides to set him free, we will welcome the move. I don't mind admitting that this is our position.

MATUTES The problem is that the question of our going to arbitration has to be discussed in the Spanish parliament, and that will take a long time. It is election year in Spain. The best thing is for Chile to go straight to The Hague without waiting for the six months to go by. It seems that one of two things will happen. Pinochet may remain for a long time in London and die there, or the British can let him go back to Chile.

VALDÉS Excuse me, Foreign Minister, there is a third possibility. He could be sent to Spain.

MATUTES No, that cannot happen. We must prevent it.

VALDÉS But you are asking for him to be extradited…

MATUTES We, as the Prime Minster has stated, want to collaborate. If you can find other legal formulae, we shall study them with the utmost attention.

INSULZA [*furious*] What more do you want us to do? You expedited the extradition request without losing a moment when, for foreign policy's sake, you could have rejected it or at least delayed it. That was the only favour we were asking of you. It has caused us serious problems.

And now, when we are proposing the arbitration possibility given in the International Agreement against Torture, which you are obliged to respect, you say you can't do it.

[*The meeting ends. The two sides leave unamicably. Outside the room, Aznar is approached by a reporter for a statement.*]

AZNAR   I have only this to say. I just hope there is a quick solution for Mr. Pinochet. Thank you. [*He moves away hurriedly.*]

Scene 5   *The garden of the house in Wentworth Estate, Surrey, where Pinochet is under house arrest. 13 July 1999. Pinochet has been prepared for an interview with a Conservative London newspaper by his Chilean and British advisers. They are worried he might voice his real opinions and damage his image. Pinochet appears in the garden from inside the house, dressed in a dark blue suit, blue and white striped shirt, and tasteful silk tie, salmon, pink, and black. He shakes hands with the two journalists. One of them, the woman, is pregnant. He greets the woman interpreter.*

PINOCHET   Are you from Bilbao?

INTERPRETER   No, I'm not, but I am a Basque.

PINOCHET   Do you know that I have Basque ancestors?

INTERPRETER   Yes, and do you know that your second surname, Ugarte, means *island* in Basque?

PINOCHET   Oh, really?

[*All sit down round a table in the garden. Pinochet puts a book with blue covers on it. The interpreter sits on his left, because Pinochet is deaf in his right ear.*]

PINOCHET   [*To the journalists. His voice, although hardly more than a hoarse whisper, is peculiarly high.*] They have kidnapped me. They should have given me advance warning of what was about to happen so that I could leave. That is what an honorable person would have done.

FEMALE JOURNALIST   Senator Pinochet, according to the Rettig Report produced under the presidency of Patricio Aylwin, a former supporter of yours, 3,197 people were killed in Chile during your mandate. [*Pinochet is silent.*]

MALE JOURNALIST   Have you ever done anything that could justify the accusation of your having committed 'crimes against humanity'?

PINOCHET   Never. [*Opens the blue book and reads out loud from it: 'It is forbidden to apply any illegal constraint on a person.'*] This is in the Constitution of Chile, which I had passed in 1980.

MALE JOURNALIST   But a lot of people have accused you of ordering torture, killings and disappearances.

PINOCHET   At that moment I had no control over what others were doing. To say what you have said is a total slander! [*Bangs the table with his fist. His aides look flustered.*]

MALE JOURNALIST   So you are saying that you never gave orders to torture or kill anybody.

PINOCHET   [*putting his elbow on the blue book and rubbing the book with it*] Look, I'm going to answer you with a saying we have in Chile. 'You don't rub out with your elbow what you have written with your hand.'

PINOCHET AIDE   The General means that he was not going to order people to do things that he himself had forbidden.

FEMALE JOURNALIST   But Colonel Manuel Contreras, the former head of DINA, has declared in court that he did nothing without your authorization.

[*Pinochet's aides whisper in consternation amongst themselves.*]

PINOCHET It is difficult to reply to that question because there are many things that I ordered him to do. But, what were they? I had to exercise power. He could never say that I was in charge of DINA because it was under the orders and supervision of the entire Junta, the four members of the Junta. And I would like you to realize this: the chief of the Army always asks: 'What are you going to do?' The question of 'how'?, 'how am I going to do it?' is a matter for the intelligence chief more than for the Army chief. This is something that civilians do not understand.

PINOCHET AIDE I think the General is rather tired and the interview should stop here. But I am sure he would welcome 'photo opportunities'. That is your phrase in English, is it not?

[*Photographers appear and prepare to take pictures of Pinochet and his sons, daughters, and six grandchildren present.*]

FEMALE JOURNALIST Thank you, Senator Pinochet. You have been most helpful.

PINOCHET You have asked some delicate questions. You are in a delicate state yourself and have to take care of yourself. It's wonderful to have a family, isn't it? [*He shakes hands with the two journalists and they move off.*]

Scene 6 *The same two journalists. Sitting on a park bench near the Wentworth Estate house.*

FEMALE JOURNALIST Those family portraits of Pinochet the photographers did. His hoarse voice. Does a bell ring?

MALE JOURNALIST Marlon Brando as Don Vito Corleone in *The Godfather*. And he even told us his e-mail address was 'Condor'. Do you remember?

FEMALE JOURNALIST Ah, 'Operation Condor', the general hunting down of leftists in the Southern Cone area. And then he systematically denies any crimes. He appointed the head of DINA himself a couple of months after the coup. You know Contreras, the one who's in jail now? They had a briefing every day over breakfast. Did you notice his fingers? Like a butcher's.

MALE JOURNALIST I don't think our paper's most prominent supporter would thank you for that remark. She hasn't a bad word to say about him. According to her, he 'saved democracy'.

FEMALE JOURNALIST Butcher's hands. You know

who Pinochet reminds me of? Macbeth.

MALE JOURNALIST Who killed his king through 'vaulting ambition'. You certainly have a point there. I know the play almost by heart. We did it at school, and I've been enthralled by it ever since. Allende was Pinochet's Duncan. You know, although a Marxist, Allende was a decent man. A gentleman Marxist, if you like. Macduff says that Duncan was 'a most sainted king'.

FEMALE JOURNALIST But these gentlemen Marxists were very dangerous. They opened the doors for the savage ones to rush in. That's why Nixon and Kissinger were dead set against Allende.

MALE JOURNALIST I suppose you know that nobody, least of all Allende, suspected that Pinochet was a plotter till the coup took place? Pinochet had helped put the tank coup of June 29 down. At the beginning of the Shakespeare play, Macbeth had already proved himself by polishing off several of Duncan's enemies. First, 'the merciless Macdonwald, worthy to be a rebel', with his 'kerns and gallowglasses from the western isles'.

FEMALE JOURNALIST 'Kerns and gallowglasses', hee, hee.

MALE JOURNALIST Rowdy Celts. In the Chilean

scenario, the major who led the tank uprising was a 'Fatherland and Freedom' man, the Chilean fascists. There are your 'kerns and gallowglasses'. Anyway, Macbeth 'unseam'd' his man 'from the nave to the chaps, And fix'd his head upon our battlements.' Then he dealt with the Norwegians and their ally the thane of Cawdor. No wonder poor old Duncan expressed 'great happiness' at having such a man in his ranks. Actually, it was General Prats who led the resistance to the tank coup, personally disarming some of the commanders. Pinochet merely backed him up, with a couple of other loyal generals. But it made him look good. And Pinochet had sworn loyalty to Allende several times. It's in Prats' diary. You know what the Bard says about Macbeth?

FEMALE JOURNALIST Go on.

MALE JOURNALIST
'This tyrant, whose sole name blisters our tongues,
Was once thought honest.'

FEMALE JOURNALIST Superb. And wasn't Macbeth a great flatterer of King Duncan? Before murdering him.

MALE JOURNALIST Yes. How does it go? [*A short pause while he recollects*]
'The service and the loyalty I owe,
In doing it, pays itself. Your highness' part

Is to receive our duties: and our duties
Are to your throne and state, children and servants;
Which do but what they should, by doing every thing
Safe toward your love and honour.'

FEMALE JOURNALIST If I remember rightly,
Macbeth hesitated a lot before murdering Duncan.

MALE JOURNALIST Yes.
'We will proceed no further in this business:
He hath honour'd me of late, and I have bought
Golden opinions from all sorts of people.'

Although Pinochet himself now says that he had been
plotting against Allende for some months before the
coup, there is evidence that he only made up his mind a
couple of days before. That's why no one suspected him.
After all, Allende had made him commander-in-chief of
the Chilean Army, the top job for him. But he must have
seen the opportunity to go even further. Macbeth had the
witches urging him on. Who were Pinochet's witches?
[*Pauses*] Of course, it's so obvious. All those upper-class
women in the pots and pans demonstrations. And, to cap
it all, there's a Lady Macbeth in the cast.

FEMALE JOURNALIST Lady Pinochet? Lucía
Hiriart de Pinochet?

MALE JOURNALIST Yes. An American journalist

told me the CIA made a report on Pinochet and his family two years before the coup. Pinochet was the commander of the Santiago garrison then, and it described him as totally immersed in the new field of security, public order and political events, and clearly enjoying the feeling of being important. He was perceived as a 'narrow-gauged military man' with a mild and friendly character. The CIA, which was trawling around for plotters to overthrow Allende, concluded that Pinochet would not lead any coup, but that his wife was already turning against the government. One of their sons was married to a woman in the National Party. In 1973, apparently, Lucía Pinochet was one of the women who publicly called Prats 'Allende's lackey'.

FEMALE JOURNALIST So she was one of the witches and Lady Macbeth at the same time. What the hell were Allende's security services doing then? My God! Neither of us, nor our paper, were exactly supporters of Allende, but what this man did was hideous. And the Baroness is backing him to the hilt.

MALE JOURNALIST After Macbeth kills Duncan, he feels remorse, but is egged on by Lady Macbeth. I never heard Pinochet show remorse for what he did. He is either denying all knowledge of the executions and torture, or trying to put the blame on subordinates. You've heard of the 'Caravan of Death'?

FEMALE JOURNALIST   Yes, I have. Pinochet sending one of his generals around the country as his lord chief executioner of former leftist officials. It's all coming out now. What was the name of that man?

MALE JOURNALIST   Stark. Arellano Stark.

FEMALE JOURNALIST   But tell me. Is there a Banquo?

MALE JOURNALIST   [*laughing*] A Banquo, a Banquo? Let's see. How about General Leigh, the Air Force commander? After the coup, he objected to Pinochet making himself head of the Junta and then President of Chile. He wasn't murdered, though I did hear that somebody made an attempt on his life. Pinochet eventually forced him off the Junta. But lucky him. He's still alive.

FEMALE JOURNALIST   I wonder what Tony Blair's going to do? Will he really give Pinochet what he deserves now he's got him here? Turn him over to the Spanish Macduffs? They're the only ones in a position to play that role. The Chilean Macduffs can't. In public Blair is all against your man. But you know how slippery he is.

MALE JOURNALIST   The Baroness has a soft spot for Blair. He'll have to go against her if he wants to give Pinochet the chop.

FEMALE JOURNALIST   Ah, New Labour. Lefty yuppies. How sweet power is to them. Certain of them even hobnob with the royal family. I think that in the end the Baroness will get her way, however much Blair insults Pinochet in speeches at Labour Party conferences. He does it to get a roar from the peasants.

MALE JOURNALIST   Oh, I even think the peasants' leader can be won over.

FEMALE JOURNALIST   Peasants' leader?

MALE JOURNALIST   Read your Shakespeare, my dear.

FEMALE JOURNALIST   Not Wat Tyler, no. Oh yes, the other one. Our delightful Home Secretary.

MALE JOURNALIST   [*smiles*] Exactly. Mine host at the top of Hampstead Hill. [*They laugh.*]

Scene 7   *October 8, 1999. Jeff, a Labour Party MP married to Rosa, a Chilean woman, is at his home in London discussing the final verdict in the extradition case versus Pinochet with his wife and friends. They are celebrating.*

JEFF   My friends, I can't say what a happy day this is

for us all. Especially for Rosa, my wife, who suffered personally under Pinochet, as did so many of her friends and comrades. Finally, the British legal system has shown it is worth something. Pinochet is to be extradited to Spain.

ROSA They'll punish him there, no doubt about it. Public opinion there is much more against the old bastard than it is here. Quite a few Spaniards got caught up in the repression, even priests.

JEFF Now it's in the Home Secretary's hands. He can still decide to stop Pinochet being sent there. I'm a bit worried that they might do that. There's been a hell of a lot of pressure on the government to return him to Chile.

ROSA Yes, dear, but I don't think the Home Secretary and Prime Minister could face their back-benchers if they did that. Especially after all those statements they made in public attacking the beast. Even recently, Blair was still having a go at him. Remember what he said at the Party Conference at Bournemouth. What was it he called the Tories?

GREY-HAIRED MAN 'The party of the uneatable, the unspeakable and the unelectable.' Lifted the whole thing from Oscar Wilde. Typical politician's trick. All those fox-hunting Tories demonstrating outside the conference must have given him the idea. Or maybe his spin-doctor.

ROSA The unspeakable was Pinochet. The only political prisoner in Britain, the Tories are calling him.

GREY-HAIRED MAN Yes. But 'unspeakable' could mean the opposite of what we are all hoping for. It may be code for 'I'm going to wash my hands of this problem.' He may be insinuating that Pinochet is so appalling that he can't be dealt with here in Europe. The Spanish politicians don't want Pinochet there. Aznar, Felipe González, and so on. They're hoping Straw will get them off the hook by stopping the extradition. The Chilean government could stymie Spanish capital invested in Chile and stop buying Spanish weaponry. Aznar had to let the extradition proceedings take their course because he didn't want to be tarred with a pro-Pinochet brush, being an ex-supporter of Franco. The People's Party! What a name for that crowd! And Felipe González is even worse. And a socialist to boot. You know what he called Judge Garzón? 'Tarzan', and 'Rambo'. He's jealous because the spotlight's no longer on him now that he's out of power.

JEFF You may be right, George. I hope to God not. All Blair's rousing speeches at the conferences may well be just for the great unwashed. But Garzón's certainly a battler, a man of principle. He's going after the Argentinian generals as well. Very Quixotic.

GREY-HAIRED MAN In a world run by Sancho Panzas.

JEFF [*laughing*] Do you think I'm a Sancho Panza?

GREY-HAIRED MAN Of course I don't. But you're a rare breed.

JEFF That's why I'm not in the inner circles of power. It's not people like me that run the world. I'm just on the outside, making loud noises.

ROSA Very beautiful loud noises, darling. That's why I married you. [*Kisses him*]

JEFF Thank you, my love. Garzón has a lot of popular support in Spain. And he's being advised by that ex-aide of Allende. What's his name? The one that escaped the coup.

ROSA Joan Garcés. The Valencian.

JEFF Yes, that's him. He came over here for the hearing, and I was introduced to him. Nice fellow. My age. He must have been young when he was Allende's adviser. I wonder how much he knew about Chile. I hear Pinochet's obsessed with him. He only let him go back to Spain from his refuge in the Spanish Embassy because he wanted Franco's support.

GREY-HAIRED MAN Strange, isn't it. Franco, the Pinochet of his time, trying to save a Marxist.

JEFF Only because he was a Spanish citizen. And perhaps even Franco had evolved a little in the direction of a civilised human being. Or maybe he saw some political advantage in it. You know what I heard Pinochet's wife said about Garcés?

ROSA 'God knows what would have happened to him if he hadn't escaped.'

JEFF He would certainly have been shot. Or tortured. Or both.

ROSA Like so many close to Allende. [*A knock on the door. Rosa goes to open it. A plump, rubicund man with a cockney accent comes in, carrying a bottle of champagne.*] It's Phil.

PHIL Great, ain't it? They finally nailed the old bugger. I got some champagne to celebrate.

GREY-HAIRED MAN We were just talking about that. We're not so sure. Even the people in power now in Chile, the democratic coalition, including socialists, want Pinochet sent back to Chile. They're afraid of the armed forces upsetting the transition to democracy. I take their point, but I'm pig-headed enough to be one of those who say '*fiat justitia, et pereat mundus*'.

PHIL You always were one for wrapping things up in

fancy words, you old intellectual. You should try getting your hands dirty in the bread-and-butter work.

GREY-HAIRED MAN Going round doors, that sort of thing, eh. Talking to Mr. and Mrs. Bloggs.

PHIL Exactly. You couldn't give them that mouthful you've just given us, old cock. What did you mean?

GREY-HAIRED MAN Justice has to be done, even if the world goes to pot.

PHIL Well, we agree on that. But some of the nobs in our party are shifting their ground on Pinochet. Mandy, for example. When David Frost interviewed him a year ago, at the beginning of the whole business, he said the idea that such a brutal dictator as Pinochet can hide behind diplomatic immunity was 'gut-wrenching'. Gut-wrenching. Now he's saying it's an affair to be decided in Chile.

JEFF Alastair had a word with him, I heard. Told him he'd put his foot in it with 'gut-wrenching'. And then, he has certain unsavoury friends.

PHIL That Chilean woman who lived here in the sixties. Lucía someone. A friend of Camilla and the Prince. Rumour has it that she was the Prince's first real girlfriend. A big supporter of Pinochet. She was the one who told the Pinochet crowd about Lord Hoffman's wife working for Amnesty.

JEFF And got the Lord's first verdict on Pinochet overturned, because Lord Hoffman was 'biased'. 'Biased' because his wife worked for a human rights organization. What do they want?

PHIL Little Lord Fauntleroys. Or Franco supporters. But old Paxman on TV was good, wasn't he, as usual. Asking: 'What did it matter?' Quite right.

JEFF Blair and Straw are under tremendous pressure. Not only from the Iron Lady, either. You would expect it from her, being so friendly with Pinochet.

GREY-HAIRED MAN I think her arguments were very crude, even for a right-wing Tory. All that business about Pinochet helping the UK in the Falklands war, pure jingoism. Then that human rights abuses had been committed by both sides. I've never heard a shred of evidence for that.

ROSA That's what the Santa Cruz woman dreamed up. Saying torture had started under President Allende, poor man. A decent person like him.

GREY-HAIRED MAN Look where it got him, being decent. The argument about preserving the new democracy in Chile I understand. The next President there may be a socialist. A socialist of the nineties, though. The Che Guevara days are well past, thank God. A democratic socialist. But I hear the Iron Lady's alarmed. Her idea of democracy is Pinochet in power. Do you remember what she said? That he had brought democracy to Chile. As well as prosperity.

PHIL After murdering his boss, the legally elected president, who never broke the rules of the constitution.

JEFF There's another name for Pinochet: Judas.

GREY-HAIRED MAN And now poor Judas is weak and infirm and an old man, they say. Even the Vatican wants Pinochet back in his own country. To say nothing of the Archbishop of Canterbury.

PHIL The Save Judas Campaign. They've come a long way in two thousand years, haven't they? What happened to Judas in the Bible, George?

GREY-HAIRED MAN He hanged himself. Another version says he burst. But this one is still alive at eighty-two.

PHIL 'Only the good die young.' [*Laughter*] Anyway. Let's hope for the best. I'm going to open my champagne. [*He does so, giving everyone a glass. To the*

MP] Now, Jeff, you were going to give us a report on the extradition hearing.

JEFF   Fine, here goes. As you know, I sat through the whole lot. Fascinating stuff. [*A knock on the door. Rosa goes to open it. A small dark man comes into the living room.*] Oh, hello, Daniel. Daniel is an old party comrade of Rosa's. [*Everybody goes to shake his hand.*] Daniel, I'm going to report on the extradition hearing. Rosa can help you out you if there's anything you don't understand. [*Everybody sits down after Daniel is given a glass.*]

JEFF   Well, the Pinochet lawyer argued that his client was an object of political persecution, and that under the European Extradition Agreement, a person could not be punished for his race, religion, nationality or political opinions.

PHIL   Okay, but he was being prosecuted for torture and murder.

JEFF   The lawyer on our side started by saying that the Bow Street court did not have to decide on Pinochet's guilt. The only thing to be proved was that in Spain he was being accused of the crimes. He mentioned the torture techniques used by the Chilean secret police. Electric shocks to the vagina, a steel tube up a man's backside, people being interrogated naked, beating bodies that were hanging up, the use of hallucinogenic

drugs. The whole caboodle you already know about. He
gave many names and cases of specific people. He said
Spain had jurisdiction for putting Pinochet on trial
despite none of the victims being Spanish, or the crimes
having not been committed in Spain.

GREY-HAIRED MAN   But there were Spanish
victims. Even priests.

JEFF   Yes, but their cases and the cases of many others
happened before the Anti-Torture Treaty was signed by
the UK and Spain. We are only now talking about people
who got the treatment after 1988. Unfortunately, Pinochet
cannot be tried in Europe for crimes previous to that. And
that means the majority of the atrocities. But the House
of Lords, by six to one, finally declared that he could be
extradited for 34 cases of conspiracy to torture and
torture. There is also the question of the 'disappeared',
something like 1,200 people whose bodies have not been
found.

PHIL   So even without people who could be accused of
human rights prejudices, they nailed him.

JEFF   The defence argued that Judge Garzón was
politically biased and an impostor. An impostor? I
wonder who thought that one up. Spain as a country was
accused of loathing Pinochet. The lawyer also argued that
there were no proofs that Pinochet had ordered the

crimes. You can't have a weaker argument than that. They were really scraping the bottom of the barrel.

ROSA I was tortured myself. God knows how many others were.

JEFF The Pinochet barrister said that although Spain had ratified the United Nations Convention on Torture, it had not yet included torture as offence for trial under Spanish law wherever the torture may have occurred. Spain had to prove either that the crimes had been committed there, or that they had been committed on Spaniards or that the accused was a Spaniard. Also that Pinochet could only be tried in Spain if he had been on Spanish soil and arrested there. He concluded by saying that Pinochet is here, not in Spain, and that torture is not a crime for extradition because it is not punished in Spain.

PHIL Pathetic. Who was the magistrate?

JEFF Ronald Bartle. He was the one in the Guildford bombings case, where the police were accused of fabricating evidence. He ordered the case against the police to be shelved.

GREY-HAIRED MAN Hmm.

JEFF Oh, there was another argument. That Pinochet

never knew about torture in these cases because in 1988 he lost the referendum, and the transition to democracy had started. That's also a very poor argument because he stayed on as head of the army until last year. For ten more years. And then the barrister said that only one of the cases out of the 34 should be examined, of a 17-year-old boy who died after torture. This was a simple case of police brutality, which continues in Chile ten years after the democratic regime began. Police brutality occurs everywhere, he said. Here, in Spain, everywhere. Not only in Chile.

PHIL   Anything else? This is pathetic stuff.

JEFF   Yes. And there is something even more incredible. He cited the case of a youth who died after electric shock treatment. He said that there could not have been suffering and severe pain, that is, torture, because his death was caused instantaneously.

PHIL   That beats the lot.

JEFF   He also claimed Pinochet was protected by diplomatic immunity. But they had a whole lot more tricks up their sleeve. Pinochet's health. His defence argued that he should not be present at the final hearing, when Bartle gave his verdict. I expect you heard that he has had the last rites. The *Daily Telegraph* took good care to report that one. But Bartle insisted he should be present. However, he agreed to hear arguments against this from the defence team.

PHIL And they pulled out all the stops.

JEFF Exactly. They said Pinochet was very tired, urinating frequently, and having dizzy spells. One day he fainted. On another, he had a small stroke. He had lost his recent memory. And it was after a second fainting fit they called in a priest. There was another stroke. One of his doctors said that if he appeared in court, it would be very tense for him and predicted yet another stroke in the following six weeks.

GREY-HAIRED MAN Almost a corpse, eh?

JEFF Exactly. So the magistrate finally gave way and allowed him not to appear on the final day.

PHIL Thatcher is going off about Marxist conspiracies, a Labour kidnapping, and the fabrications of a Marxist Spanish judge working with a whole network of other Marxist devils, including Allende's old political adviser. On the one hand she is saying that Pinochet is innocent, then on the other that the left wants revenge. Revenge for what, if he is innocent?

GREY-HAIRED MAN Right.

PHIL The lady wants justice, not revenge, she says. And justice for her is simple: free Pinochet. [*Imitating Thatcher's voice*] 'Perhaps he will die here, as the only political prisoner in this country. Or in Spain, awaiting a despicable parody of justice.'

GREY-HAIRED MAN Boo-hoo.

JEFF Anyway, today the magistrate decided that Pinochet can be extradited for trial in Spain. Those 34 cases of torture occurring after December 1988 are relevant and he can be accused for them. He quoted the extradition law, which defines a crime for extradition as behaviour in the territory of a foreign state, which, had it occurred in the UK, would be a crime punishable by a jail sentence of twelve months or more. And the Spanish High Court had determined that what Pinochet is accused of are extraditable offences. Bartle said he had to respect that verdict. Then that it had been finally decided by the House of Lords judges that Pinochet had no immunity from prosecution.

PHIL So he's all set for Spain.

JEFF Apparently. But Bartle made a point of saying that the matter was in the hands of the Home Secretary. *He* has the final decision.

PHIL It's not only Straw. It's the whole thing behind him.

JEFF Yes.

GREY-HAIRED MAN I'm worried. Blair and Co. are essentially fixers. Will they make an alliance with Aznar, Felipe González, and the other Sancho Panzas?

JEFF There's one unfortunate fact. You know the Baroness quite likes Blair. I heard over the grapevine that she also quite approves of Felipe González, in spite of him being a socialist. And Felipe González has always been dead set on getting Pinochet back to Chile. He's made it public several times, in Europe and in Chile. He even said that if the whole business of Pinochet was not political, he was in the wrong business. Blair's public stance has always been the opposite. The whole thing had to go through the courts. It was not political.

GREY-HAIRED MAN Despite what Lamont and Thatcher are saying.

JEFF Well, now it's out of the hands of the courts. And in the hands of the politicians.

GREY-HAIRED MAN Despite not being 'political'. Draw your own conclusions.

PHIL Yes, God forbid.

ROSA And Pinochet, the old devil, is repeating he is

innocent of all crimes. If he's sent back, he'll never be tried in Chile. The Armed Forces won't allow it.

JEFF   The whole thing stinks. We'll just have to hope for the best. I need another drink.

ALL   Hear, hear.

Scene 8   *Five months later, March 2, 2000. 7 p.m. The Home Secretary's decision to free Pinochet has been announced earlier in the day. A small, almost empty café in a London suburb. Daniel and Rosa are talking animatedly in Spanish. The café door opens and they turn their heads. Jeff walks in, sees the two and sits down at their table.*

ROSA   Hullo, Jeff. We've been waiting ages. Tell us how it went in the Commons. How did Jack Straw justify his decision?

JEFF   It was all window-dressing, of course. Blah, blah, blah. I've been in politics long enough to know how they do it. The writing was on the wall when Straw started saying a few weeks ago that he was 'inclined' to free Pinochet. Blair was impatient to get the whole thing settled. The secret medical reports made by British doctors gave Straw grounds for saying that Pinochet was not fit to stand trial. I understand he's already out of the country. [*Daniel says something to Rosa.*]

ROSA Daniel's very upset. He can hardly believe it. To let the man off the hook after it went through all those British courts. And a Labour government, too.

JEFF It looked bad when Thatcher called Straw 'a very just man' after his first announcement about his 'inclination'. She knew then it was all tied up. Ah, the way of the world. Damn them all.

DANIEL *No lo puedo creer.*

JEFF I know, Daniel, but you don't understand politics here.

ROSA So what happened in the Commons?

JEFF Well, Straw got up on his hind legs and announced that earlier today Pinochet had been taken under police escort from Wentworth to RAF Waddington, where a Chilean Air Force plane was waiting to take off at 1:10 p.m. The Senator has left the jurisdiction of the United Kingdom, he said.

ROSA They weren't taking any chances, were they?

JEFF Straw said the sentence of the House of Lords judges passed on 24 March last year was a milestone in the history of human rights, whose impact had been felt beyond the United Kingdom. It would be a definitive legacy of the Pinochet case.

ROSA   Meaning what?

JEFF   You remember the case of the seven judges, after Pinochet's lawyers managed to invalidate the previous judgement in the Lords against Pinochet because Lord Hoffman's wife worked for Amnesty International. By six to one, the verdict was that torture is an international crime and that a chief of state cannot show that committing an international crime is fulfilling a function protected by international law through immunity.

[*Rosa translates for Daniel. He mutters something.*]

ROSA   Daniel says that Pinochet became chief of state after murdering his own president.

JEFF   [*ironically*] I don't think that argument ever came up. Anyway, that verdict said that Pinochet could be extradited for crimes of torture and conspiracy to torture presumably committed after December 1988. They added that political arguments of parties concerned were of no relevance, nor the convenience or inconvenience of the extradition of Pinochet to Spain.

ROSA   So it wasn't a political question, just as Blair said.

JEFF   Everything is politics, at this level. The Home Secretary said that if the extradition process continued, there would be political consequences. The military government in Chile might come back, especially if Pinochet ended up facing a court in Spain. Then he hedged, saying that in fact there was no evidence to suggest that this would occur.

ROSA   My God, what contortions.

JEFF   Having his cake and eating it, eh? But he went on to say that there was overwhelming proof that Chile and the whole of Latin America have been helped by this case to come to terms with their undemocratic past.

ROSA   What's that you say here in English. About stopping a ship by firing?

JEFF   By firing a shot across its bows. He was in fact saying that we were out to rap the knuckles of all naughty murderous dictators. But his main argument for releasing our friend was the medical one. He wasn't fit to stand trial, wouldn't understand what was going on. [*Rosa translates for Daniel, who bursts out laughing and then hides his face in his hands.*] And that because of that, a trial would be a violation of his human rights, according to the European Human Rights Convention.

ROSA   Pinochet's human rights. Anything more?

JEFF I got up and said that many people here would be
filled with shame that Pinochet had left the UK, and that
he would in all probability not be tried anywhere in the
world now.

ROSA What did Straw say?

JEFF He admitted that, but drew my attention to the
Roisin McAliskey case, where he also decided, on the
evidence of independent medical reports, that she was
unfit to stand trial in Germany because she had
psychological problems. She was accused of committing
a terrorist act there. He recalled that in that instance I had
congratulated him. The Tories were baying for his blood,
you know, but Blair was negotiating with the IRA at the
time.

ROSA You're right. It's all political.

JEFF Yes, love, unfortunately. And in this case, the
politicians have buried justice.

[*Daniel speaks to Rosa.*]

ROSA Daniel says that even Ricardo Lagos wanted
Pinochet back. And he's our new President. A good man.
He saved a lot of Chileans exiled in Argentina when
Operation Condor got going. Perhaps he can bring
Pinochet to justice. Many of the others have already been

put on trial in Chile. You know, I could be wrong about the military being solid for Pinochet. Some of the new generation may even be ashamed of him.

DANIEL [*recovering his spirits and even laughing*] Money. Pinochet. DINA. *Cuentas de millones de dólares en los Estados Unidos. Una parte de la derecha chilena está con vergüenza de Pinochet.*

ROSA He says some of the right are thinking of dumping Pinochet. There's an embarrassing financial scandal involving a DINA account in the USA with evidence that Pinochet siphoned off millions from this account for himself.

JEFF I get it. They don't care about him massacring people on the left, whom they call communists, but they draw the line at sticky fingers. They want honest murderers.

ROSA That's our upper class in Chile.

JEFF There is a ray of hope, then.

ROSA You know, I think there is.

FINAL CURTAIN

After his release from British custody and return to Chile, Pinochet lived on for nearly six years, dying at the age of 91 on December 10, 2006. On his ninety-first birthday, just two weeks before his death, he issued a statement taking 'full political responsibility' for his actions. Although many charges were brought against him through the Chilean legal system, his lawyers were to plead successfully that he was physically and mentally incapable of standing trial. His funeral was conducted by the Chilean military and was not allowed state honours by the Chilean President, Michelle Bachelet, whose father, Air Force General Alberto Bachelet, had remained loyal to President Allende and been imprisoned and tortured, dying a few months after his arrest. Pinochet was never sentenced for any of his crimes.

This first edition of "Allende / Pinochet: Two Political Dramas" was produced by CBH Books in Lawrence, Massachusetts and printed in Quebec, Canada in 2007.

For comments about this publication or permission requests, please write to:
CBH Books
A division of Cambridge BrickHouse, Inc.
60 Island Street
Lawrence, MA 01840 U.S.A.